MY BILLION BIBLE DREAM

A gift from #1985

Carolyn Winslow Circle

MY Billion Bible DREAM

By

Rochunga Pudaite

with James Hefley

Thomas Nelson Publishers
Nashville • Camden • New York

ISBN 0-8407-5812-X

Library of Congress number 82–19050

Contents

Lovingly dedicated
to my
dear father and mother,
Chawnga and Daii Pudaite,
whose love and prayers inspired me
to carry the Good News
"beyond the horizons"
of the world.

Acknowledgments

I AM MOST thankful for those who helped make this book a reality—for my long-time journalist friend, Jim Hefley, who put my thoughts and ideas into readable type, for Cyndi Allison, Jim's talented artist-daughter, who provided illustrations; for my secretary, Carolyn Morse, and sons Paul and John Pudaite, who typed the manuscript on our new word processor (and our daughter Mary who cheered them on and typed one paragraph); and most of all for my dear and beloved Mawii, the sweetheart of my life, who shared so many of the experiences, corrected some of my memories, gave so many marvelous insights, and helped bring the book to completion.

There is, of course, a larger company to whom I am grateful—our supportive board members, our loyal staff, our Bibles For The World family who have faithfully stood with us, and the thousands of believers among my own Hmar people who have demonstrated in their lives the power of the Bible.

Beyond and above all those who have helped, I thank our great God who revealed Himself and His will in the Bible, who brought me from a humble bamboo house in the jungle and gave me a vision that encompasses the whole earth. To Him be honor and glory forever, to the end that His Word be given to every person on earth and that His church may be built to completeness and prepared for His coming to receive the redeemed of every tribe and nation into His heavenly presence.

ROCHUNGA PUDAITE
September, 1982

Chapter 1

The Book That Set My People Free

MAWII AND I were enjoying a much-needed vacation in Florida with two of our children, Paul and Mary. Our dear friends Ray and Edie Quiggin had invited us to spend a few days aboard their yacht. One morning after breakfast and Bible study, Ray and I left our wives to go ashore. As we were coming off the boat, Ray spotted a friend and called, "Hey, George, come and meet my friend Rochunga."

A distinguished-looking, heavy-set man, wearing a captain's cap and with flecks of gray at his temples, walked briskly toward us. When we shook hands and he learned I was from India, I saw a robust and very determined look on his face.

"From India, huh," he said quickly. "I've been to Calcutta and Bombay and all those poor cities. I never saw so many hungry, starving people in my life. Whole families living on the street. Little children with arms and legs like matchsticks. Old grandmothers picking at garbage. I came away so depressed. I wish we could find some way to help them."

"Ro is mailing Bibles to India and many other countries,"

Ray interjected. "His organization mailed over a million New Testaments last year."

George's face clouded with incredulity. "You're sending Bibles? Bibles to India? Pardon me, if I seem rude. But how can you justify mailing a million Bibles when so many people are starving to death? Take up a collection and buy food, man. You do that, and I'll be the first to contribute."

"George, I wish we could feed all the world's hungry tomorrow. But if we had fifty million dollars we could only buy breakfast for maybe one-fifth of all the hungry people in India. Before the day is over, they'd be hungry again."

"Well, no, I don't mean handouts. But I can't see that sending Bibles will help either. Somebody has to find a way to help them build industries, create jobs, get schools, so they can buy their own food. Even at that, I expect it will take them another generation to get back to normal. They've been malnourished for so long that their brains are withered and their genes deformed."

"George, the Bible can do all that," I said.

But George was not listening. He kept talking about hunger and how ridiculous he felt it was to send Bibles. He was haunted by memories of so many hungry people, maybe feeling guilty because he couldn't think of a way to help them.

Finally I held up my hand. "George," I entreated, "may I have my moment."

"Certainly. Forgive me. I got carried away. After all, you are from that part of the world."

"Yes, I come from what was once one of the most malnourished tribes of India. My grandfather was a headhunter. Have you ever heard of the Hmars?"

"Hmars . . . no, I've never heard of them."

"The Hmars are my people. Our Mongolian ancestors came from central China across the lower Himalayas and settled in northeast India. When they fought, they took heads and hung them over the doors of their bamboo huts. The British colonialists called the Hmars 'barbaric tribesmen' and said we were almost like animals. When the British tried to take over our territory our warriors fought back. The Hmars took 500 heads in one raid on a tea plantation. General Lord Roberts, the British commander, came after our men with two columns. The British killed a few, but most escaped back into the forest. That's where they were when a Welsh missionary brought the Bible.

"May I tell you about how the Bible came to us and what it did? I think you will be surprised."

"Yes, yes, go ahead," George urged.

"Watkin Roberts was a chemist in Wales when a great spiritual revival swept his area. He read Lord Roberts's account of the pursuit of the Hmar headhunters and felt God wanted him to take the Bible to the Hmars. But when he arrived on our borders, the British agent said to enter our territory was too dangerous. He found some Lushais from a tribe adjoining the Hmars and set to work to translate the Bible in the Lushai language.

"One day, missionary Roberts received a gift of five pounds, worth about twenty-five dollars in American currency, from a Christian woman in Hemstead, England. He used this money to print a few hundred copies of the Gospel of John in Lushai. Then he sent Gospels by a British runner to the chief of each village in the tribal area.

"The chief in my father's village of Senvon received one of the Gospels. A Lushai tribesman happened to be there and read the book to him. But the Lushai could not satisfactorily explain what it meant to be born again. He suggested that the chief invite the translator, Roberts, to the village.

"When Roberts asked the British agent for permission, he was told not to go. 'When I go in there, I take along a hundred soldiers for protection,' the agent said. 'I can't spare a single soldier for you!' When Roberts showed the invitation to the British official, the agent retorted, 'That's an invitation to have your head lopped off. They'll make a celebration out of you.' But Roberts found an interpreter and went."

"Go on, go on," George urged. "Did they make a celebration out of Roberts?"

"No, the chief received him graciously. But Roberts couldn't seem to help the chief understand the gospel either. After five days he was about ready to leave when his interpreter, who had been listening, took him aside and told him a story. 'When two tribes are at war,' the interpreter said, 'the side that wishes to make peace goes to a mountaintop at sunrise and beats a big war drum three times. If the other side replies before sundown by beating their war drum, that means, "come to the boundary and let's talk it over." The chief who wants to make peace kills an animal and lets the blood of the animal flow along the boundary line. Then he and his enemy place their hands on the slain animal while their spokesmen negotiate. When they reach an understanding, the chiefs embrace and share in a peace dinner. I believe that is the way you can explain how God makes peace with man,' the interpreter told Watkin Roberts.

"That evening missionary Roberts explained to the Hmar chief that God so loved the world that He sent His Son to die on the cross—the 'boundary' of sin between God and man—to make peace with man. The Bible was a record of God's treaty with man and His invitation for man to come to the boundary and accept God's sacrifice for peace.

"The chief and four other Hmars solemnly announced they wished to make peace with the great God of the Bible. Once they had done so, Roberts returned to the British outpost.

"One of those who came and accepted God's peace treaty was my father, Chawnga.

"My father became one of the first Hmar preachers. He traveled by foot and canoe all over Hmar country telling the people to come to the boundary and accept God's sacrifice for the forgiveness of their sins. He dearly loved missionary Roberts, and called him 'Mr. Youngman,' for he was only twenty-two when he came to our people. My father would tell me, 'Mr. Youngman is not like the other British. He does not demand that tribals carry his baggage. He never insists that we follow European ways. He treats us with dignity and tells us to build our own churches after the way the Bible teaches.'

"George, because my father followed Mr. Youngman, the British agent had him whipped. Mr. Youngman was ordered to leave. The other British called him a troublemaker. He left us only part of the Bible in the Lushai language.

"My father and other Hmar preachers started churches in almost every Hmar village. Thousands of our people accepted God's peace treaty with great joy. They were so tired of quarreling, fighting, drinking, and living in fear of evil spirits. When they became Christians they began living different lives. God gave them the incentive to work harder and to build schools for their children.

"George, when I was just ten, my father confided that I had been dedicated as a baby by the church elders to translate the Bible for our people. He took me to a high mountain and showed me the horizon—'where the heaven touches the earth.' If I were to go to the next mountain, he told me, there would be another, then another beyond that, for the horizon never ends. 'God's love,' he assured me, 'will go with you, my son, beyond the horizon.'

"My father escorted me ninety-six miles through dangerous jungle to a mission school. He left me there on my own. I had to round up and milk several cows every day for my keep and tuition. God helped me go all the way through college in India, one of the first ones in my tribe to do so.*

"Because I was the best-educated Hmar, my people asked me to lead their first political party. But Mr. Youngman and a missionary leader named Bob Pierce raised funds for me to get Bible training in Scotland and America so I could translate the Bible for my people. I was the first one of my people to travel abroad for education and the first to earn a master's degree.

"Mr. Youngman had founded the little Indo-Burma Pioneer Mission to help the Hmars and other tribal peoples build schools and spread the gospel to more villages. Our beloved missionary was now very old and feeble. When I finished translating the Hmar New Testament, he asked if I would take over the leadership of the mission. Mawii, my Hmar sweetheart whom I had married, and I started with the names of just 114 potential contributors. We changed the name to Partnership Mission and continued to emphasize Mr. Youngman's idea that tribal churches should develop on their own with only some financial help from Western Christians.

"George, since the Hmars got the Bible they have become one of the most advanced ethnic groups in all of India. At least ninety-five percent are Christians, worshiping in over 200 churches. Except for Mr. Youngman, the only missionary they have had is the Bible.

"Hmar population is now up to about 125,000. Eighty-five percent can read and write, a phenomenal percentage in India. They have eighty-eight church-sponsored elementary schools, seven junior highs, and four high schools—one with an enrollment of about a thousand. They even have a good hospital, staffed by Hmar doctors and nurses.

---

*You can read about my schooling in my biography, *God's Tribesman*. There is also a film on my life called *Beyond the Next Mountain*.

"Most of our people eat quite well, too. Per family income stands at about $400 a year. That isn't a lot compared to America, but it is much higher than the average income in the rest of India or Bangladesh.

"A government coffee expert says we have the best land for growing coffee in all of India. So our 'partners' in America have been helping us develop a coffee crop. We already have a half million trees and expect to have five million in just a few years. The Hmar church requires each of our village schools to have an acre of coffee for every ten pupils.

"George, do I look as if my brain is withered and my genes deformed?"

"No, you look as smart as any American, and smarter than a lot," he said.

"Do you know that I never had a glass of milk or even a boiled egg while I was in school? By the standards of the West, I was certainly malnourished. If my brain was stunted and my genes malformed, then the Bible has enlarged my brain and rearranged my genes."

"If you put it that way, I guess you're right." George conceded.

"And I am not the only one. One of our Hmars holds the rank of ambassador in the Indian Embassy in Yugoslavia. Another is the Indian chargé d'affaires in Saudi Arabia. Another is the highest ranking civil servant of India. Another is the administrator of a large state. Every year the government gives tests to select the outstanding young men for government service. Only about twenty are selected in the whole country. For several years one or two Hmars have been in each group of winners. And there is only about one Hmar for every 7,000 people in India. I know I am bragging, but I am proud of what the Bible has done for our people."

George was staring across the water in deep thought. "I never thought about the Bible along those lines," he admitted.

"The Hmars are taking the Bible to other tribes. Our evangelists have started hundreds of new churches. They have taken food to villages of other tribes caught up in famine and war."

"Amazing!" George suddenly exclaimed. "What you have been telling me is positively amazing! I suppose you can document all you have told me," he added.

"Go and see for yourself," I challenged. "Talk to Indian officials in New Delhi. The prime minister knows what the Bible has done among the Hmars. I have talked with her personally. And with Nehru, her father, when he was the prime minister. The Indian government is very proud of the Hmars, especially since some other tribes in the area have been giving them trouble. I have tried to be a peacemaker."

"Tell me about that," George requested.

"About two years ago the Indian government asked if I would undertake a peace mission. Mizo and Naga tribesmen, who had been trained for terrorism in Communist China, had been killing people and blowing up government buildings. They wanted political independence from India. The most violence had been occurring on India's Independence Day, August 15.

"I went to talk to some of the rebel leaders. I thought they trusted me because I am a Hmar and a Christian. On this Independence Day—it was in 1975—I was in the capital of the state of Mizoram, relaxing in the bedroom of the house where I was staying. A guard was supposed to be in the living room.

"Suddenly a young Mizo appeared and pushed a revolver into my chest. 'I am here to eliminate you,' he said.

"I looked him straight in the eye and said, 'I am a

Christian. I follow the Bible. I am an agent of peace. I am trying to be an influence for God and goodwill and to get the killing stopped.'

"The man just stared at me, stony faced and silent. 'Before you carry out your job, will you kneel with me and let me pray for you?' I asked. 'Then you can do whatever you must.'

"George, I closed my eyes and talked to the Lord in the Mizo language. I asked that my companion be kept from harm and not be killed and that grievances be settled so peace could come. I said, 'Lord, open the eyes of our people so they may see the beauty of their fellowman. Show them Your love. Help them learn to live in peace.'

"When we got up, he started walking away. 'Wait,' I said. 'Will you be my messenger and tell your people that I come in peace and goodwill? Tell your people not to explode any bombs today. That will be the signal that a confidence exists between us.'

"He slipped away without saying a word. I waited— listening, hoping, praying. The day passed. After dark the governor called. 'Come and join me in a celebration. This marks the beginning of goodwill. This is the first time since 1966 that a bomb has not gone off in the capital of this state.'"

"Has the rebellion stopped?" George asked.

"No, many of the problems are still there. But the violence has greatly diminished. A kind of cease-fire exists. But it would be much worse without the influence of the Bible.

"George, I have kept you too long. I, too, am grieved about the people who are starving and the wars, the murders, the rapes, and so many other terrible things happening all over the world. If you read the newspapers and watch television, you almost feel like giving up hope. You want to run and hide and never come out.

"But, George, there is hope in the Bible. It is not a magic talisman, but it shows us the way to peace with God and forgiveness. It teaches us to love and help one another.

"George, that's why I believe giving the Bible is the best investment anyone can make."

I had spoken a long time. But George still wanted to know more. "Can we keep in touch?" he requested as we parted. "I want to know more about the Bible and what you are doing."

For George and many others who have asked about the Bible, this book is written. For politicians, ambassadors, businessmen, teachers, doctors, lawyers, factory workers, and field laborers. For Christians, Buddhists, Hindus, Muslims, Jews, and Communists. For Americans, British, Indians, Chinese, Pakistanis, Japanese, Koreans, Peruvians, Lebanese, Arabs, and members of all other nationalities.

The Bible is the Book that reveals the mind of God, the heart of man, the way of salvation, and the blessedness of believers. It is the Book that tells us where we come from and where we are going. It is the Book that set my people free from economic and spiritual bondage. It is the Book that stands through the ages, the Book with universal appeal for all humanity, the Book that changes history, the Book that made America great, the Book that builds the church, and the Book for which God has given me the vision to send a free copy to a billion people around the world.

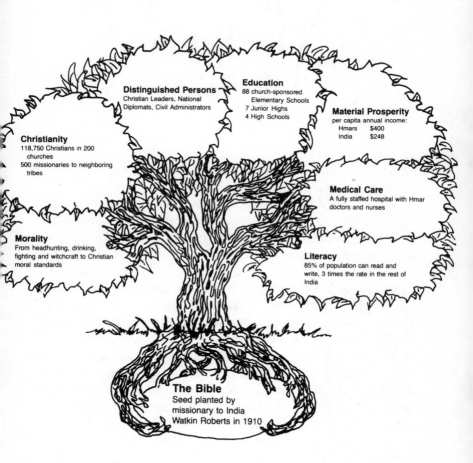

Distinguished Persons
Christian Leaders, National
Diplomats, Civil Administrators

Education
88 church-sponsored
    Elementary Schools
7 Junior Highs
4 High Schools

Material Prosperity
per capita annual income:
    Hmars $400
    India $248

Christianity
118,750 Christians in 200
    churches
500 missionaries to neighboring
    tribes

Medical Care
A fully staffed hospital with Hmar
doctors and nurses

Morality
From headhunting, drinking,
fighting and witchcraft to Christian
moral standards

Literacy
85% of population can read and
write, 3 times the rate in the rest of
India

The Bible
Seed planted by
missionary to India
Watkin Roberts in 1910

Chapter 2

The Book
That Stands

I WAS ACTUALLY flying over the land of the Bible. The KLM Super Constellation was carrying me from India to Scotland, where I was to begin training for translating the Bible into the Hmar language.

I could hardly contain my feelings when the pilot announced we were approaching the Persian Gulf and would soon be flying over Iraq, Syria, and Lebanon. Peering down at the ancestral home of Abraham and the traditional site of the Garden of Eden, I saw two wiggly blue lines—the Tigris and the Euphrates rivers—coming together in the brown desert at the head of the blue gulf. To the southwest were Israel and Jordan; straight ahead were Syria and Lebanon; beyond were Beirut and the azure Mediterranean where the apostle Paul had crossed to Greece and Rome.

Passing under me were the lands where the Book for all mankind had been written by divine inspiration—the Book expressing "the most sublime philosophy" (Sir Isaac Newton) and "our only safe guide" (Daniel Webster), "the Book of all others to read at all ages and in all conditions of human life" (John Quincy Adams), the Book which "contains all things desirable to man" (Abraham Lincoln). My heart raced at just being able to see from 39,000 feet the land where the Book that transformed my people had been written.

Some years later, after I had completed my schooling and had translated the New Testament into Hmar, I walked where Abraham, Moses, Jesus, and Paul walked. I stood at the foot of the barren, rugged mountain where it is believed Moses received the Ten Commandments. I climbed the beautiful Mount Nebo from which the great Lawgiver viewed the Promised Land. I blended in with the pilgrims at Bethlehem, traversed the dusty streets of Nazareth, and set sail on the then calm Sea of Galilee.

Later I reverently paused in the Garden of Gethsemane and felt the bark of the hoary olive trees under which Jesus may have prayed. I marched along the Way of the Cross, surveyed craggy Golgotha, and stood in awe at the empty tomb. Scenes from the Bible passed before me as I walked the sacred paths. I could hear in my imagination the prophets and apostles and our Lord Himself speaking the words that are preserved for all humanity in this Book of books.

Never has there been a book like the Bible. No book has ever matched the production schedule of the world's all-time best seller, the Bible.

No author, publisher, or editor ever planned the Bible.

No official committee sat down in the beginning to map out the production schedule of the sixty-six "books" of the Bible. The idea and schedule were conceived only in the mind of almighty God.

Jehovah, the great I AM, inspired over forty different authors and editors to produce, over a 1500-year span, the original text. The Greek word for "inspire" is *theopneustos*— *theo* meaning "God," and *pneustos,* "breathed." The same God who breathed life into man when He created man in

His own image, breathed His revelation and will into the written Word.

Only the "Alpha and Omega, the beginning and the end, the first and the last" (Rev. 22:13) could have conceived and carried out such a project. From Genesis 1 to Revelation 22, kings and rulers, nations and empires rise and fall across this Book's pages. The Bible grew portion by portion, century by century into a progressive record of God's dealings with mankind, climaxing with the redemptive intervention of God Himself for man's salvation, the birth and growth of the church, and the promise of a new heaven and a new earth where sin and suffering will be known no more and God's redeemed people will live in His presence in perfect joy and peace forever.

". . . holy men of God spake as they were moved by the Holy Ghost" (2 Pet. 1:21). The Greek word for moved is translated "borne along." The Spirit of the living God directed and protected the authors from writing errors as the Bible grew through the centuries.

They never held an editorial conference or convened a sales meeting. Matthew, Mark, Luke, and John did not confer and agree that Matthew should focus on Christ as King, Mark depict Him as Son of Man, Luke present Him as the Servant Worker, and John emphasize His divinity. Nor did Paul and James meet over lunch in an inn and decide that Paul should emphasize doctrine, and James, practical Christian living.

The Holy Spirit allowed the human authors to express their unique personalities and write, for the most part, within their own background and experiences. So Solomon in Proverbs reflected on practical lessons learned from life, David sang in Psalms of deep spiritual feelings and emotions, and Luke graphically recorded in Acts the expansion of the first century church as he observed it on missionary journeys with Paul. But all "spoke from God" (2 Pet. 1:21 RSV).

Scripture declares in hundreds of places, "The Lord said," "God spake," "These are the words of the Lord," and "The Lord commanded." Evangelist Billy Graham observes: "Either God did speak to these men as they wrote by inspiration, or they were the most consistent liars the earth ever saw."

The most important church leaders and theologians through the ages agree that the Bible is uniquely inspired by God.

Clement, the leader of the church at Rome and a contemporary of the apostles: "The Scriptures are the true words of the Holy Spirit."

Tertullian, the leading defender of Christianity during the second and third centuries: "The Scriptures are the writings of God."

Augustine, the most influential Christian writer since the apostle Paul: "Not one of the authors [of Scripture] erred in writing anything at all."

Martin Luther, the spearhead of the Reformation: "No other doctrine should be proclaimed in the Church than the pure Word of God, that is, the Holy Scriptures."

Edward J. Young, renowned Old Testament scholar of the twentieth century: "These Scriptures possess Divine authority and trustworthiness and . . . are free from error."

Sir Isaac Newton, discoverer of the law of gravity and acclaimed by many to be the greatest scientist of all history: "I find more sure marks of authenticity in the Bible than in any profane history whatsoever."

Sir Winston Churchill, the prime minister who snatched England from the jaws of defeat in World War II: "We rest with assurancce upon the impregnable rock of Holy Scripture."

At least six great witnesses attest to the power and inspiration of the Bible. First, there is *the witness of unity among diversity.*

A book with many authors today usually calls for the writers to be educated in the same field and share similar experiences. Not so the Bible. Kings and peasants, priests and soldiers, scholars and professional men served as God's instruments in writing the Bible. God "spoke" to them "in many ways" (Heb. 1:1 NASB), as they wrote in three different languages—Hebrew, Aramaic, and Greek.

The Old Testament was probably penned on dried animal skins, with some portions perhaps carved on stone. The New Testament was likely written on thin, delicate papyrus paper. The human authors wrote during prosperity and famine, war and peace, in palaces and in prisons, at home and on long journeys. They followed different styles and presented God's revelation in such different types of literature as biography, philosophy, theology, poetry, prophecy, ethnology, genealogy, romance, and adventure.

Yet a beautiful unity envelops and entwines all this diversity. A marvelous progression of history unfolds, clearly pointing toward a date with divine destiny, from Genesis to Revelation.

At the center of this marvelous unity is God's love-gift of Himself, "the Word" who "was made flesh, and dwelt among us" (John 1:14). So the Testaments are complementary rather than contradictory. The Old Testament predicts and prepares the way for His first coming. The New Testament proclaims the Savior's birth, ministry, death, resurrection, and promised return. As an unknown poet wrote:

> The New is in the Old concealed;
> The Old is in the New revealed;
> The New is in the Old contained;
> The Old is in the New explained.

The Messiah's image illumines each book. In Genesis, He is the Seed of the woman; in Exodus, the Passover Lamb; in Ruth, the kinsman Redeemer; in Job, the living Redeemer; in Psalms, the Good Shepherd; in Proverbs, the personification of wisdom; in Ecclesiastes, the meaning of life; in Isaiah, the Child of a virgin, "Wonderful Counselor," and "man of sorrows . . . wounded for our transgressions" (7:14; 9:6; 53:3, 5 NASB); in Amos, the Judge of nations; in Zechariah, the King riding upon a colt; in Matthew, the King of the Jews; in Acts, the Spirit that empowers the church; in Romans, the Justifier of all who accept His redemption; in Colossians, our "hope of glory" (1:27); in 1 Peter, the Chief Cornerstone of the church; in Revelation, the Victor over Satan, sin, and death, and in the final chapter, the glorious destiny of the redeemed.

Second, there is *the witness of fulfilled prophecies.* Hundreds and hundreds of predictions have been perfectly and exactly fulfilled, and many others have partially come to pass. Biblical prophecies compass thousands of years and relate to individuals, cities, nations, empires, the earth, the universe, events, destructive judgments, cleansing revivals, the kingdom of God, and Jesus Christ, King of Kings. Our so-called prophets of today cannot begin to equal the Bible in its record of prophecies fulfilled.

Take the once great city of Tyre on the Mediterranean Sea. The walls of Tyre towered 150 feet high and were just as broad. Built before Israel entered the Promised Land, Tyre stood for centuries as one of the world's greatest trading ports. But Tyre rejected God and practiced idolatry. The Lord spoke through Ezekiel in the sixth century B.C.:

'Behold, I am against you, O Tyre, and I will bring up many nations against you, as the sea brings up its waves. And they will destroy the walls of Tyre and break down her towers; and I will scrape her debris from her and make her a bare rock. She will be a place for the spreading of nets in the midst of the sea . . . and she will become spoil for the nations' (26:3–5 NASB).

This and other prophecies about Tyre literally came true. Nation after nation besieged Tyre. Egypt captured and held the city for a short time then, as Ezekiel predicted, Babylon launched an attack and destroyed the fortress. Many inhabitants fled to an island a half-mile from the mainland and built a second Tyre.

The new Tyre became a great port city and endured until Alexander the Great built a stone and timber causeway from the ruins of the old city to the island and conquered all. Today only the causeway stones remain to tell us that a city was there. Lebanese fishermen dry their nets on these stones, just as God predicted they would.

And what of Nineveh, built by Nimrod, the great-grandson of Noah? The prophet Nahum warned: "Whatever you devise against the LORD, He will make a complete end of it. . . . 'Behold, I am against you,' declares the LORD of hosts. 'I will burn up her chariots in smoke, a sword will devour your young lions . . .'" (1:9; 2:13 NASB). Zephaniah predicted:

He will make Nineveh a desolation,
Parched like the wilderness. . . .
This is the exultant city
Which dwells securely,
Who says in her heart,
"I am, and there is no one besides me."
How she has become a desolation,
A resting place for beasts!
Everyone who passes by her will hiss
And wave his hand in contempt (2:13,15 NASB).

When these and other prophecies were written, Nineveh was the queen city of the most powerful nation in the world. Hundred-foot walls, punctuated by 1500 towers, each 200 feet high, encircled and protected the city sixty miles around. It seemed incredible that Nineveh should fall. But it was destroyed by invading hordes in 612 B.C. The attackers cleverly diverted the Khoser River into the city, where it dissolved the sun-dried brick buildings. Nahum precisely predicted just this. "The gates of the rivers are opened,/And the palace is dissolved" (2:6 NASB).

I have not space to tell of prophecies fulfilled in the destruction of Babylon and other once-great nations. Even more remarkable are predictions of happenings among the Jews, hundreds of years before they occurred. The birth of the promised nation, the victories in Canaan, the fall of Israel into idolatry, the destruction of Jerusalem and the temple, the captivity, and the return of remnants from exile to rebuild Jerusalem and the temple were all predicted long before in the Old Testament. And in the New Testament, our Lord foretold incredible judgments on Jerusalem which were fulfilled when the Roman army under Titus besieged and starved the Jews into submission. The gruesome results are graphically predicted in Luke 19:43,44 and Matthew 24:2, some forty years before they happened.

The wonder of the rebirth of the modern state of Israel is a marvel to many Christians who point to Bible passages predicting this amazing event. Who could have believed that, after over 2,000 years of wandering among the nations and indescribable persecutions, Israel would be reestablished as a nation?

"Give me a single, definitive proof that the Bible is true," Frederick the Great of Prussia asked his chaplain. "The Jews, your Majesty, the Jews," the clergyman replied. This was two centuries before Israel again became a nation.

Most amazing of all are the prophecies about the Lord Jesus. Scores of details about his life, death, resurrection, ascension, and second coming were written centuries before He was born. Predictions include His ancestry (Is. 9:7), birthplace (Mic. 5:2), manner of birth (Is. 7:14), infancy (Hos. 11:1), manhood (Is. 40:11), character (Is. 9:6), career (Is. 35:5,6), reception (Zech. 9:9), rejection (Mic. 5:1), death (Ps. 22:16), burial (Is. 53:9), resurrection (Ps. 16:10), ascension (Ps. 68:18), and many other facts that could not possibly have been known by human means.

Dr. E. Schuyler English, chairman of the New Scofield Reference Bible and editor-in-chief of the Pilgrim Bible, notes the fulfillment of over twenty Old Testament predictions relating to the death of Christ alone!

Third, *the witness of archaeology to the life and times of bygone people of the sacred record* adds more luster to the wonder of the Bible.

As a boy I was fascinated by picture carvings on the tombstones of long-departed Hmars in jungle cemeteries. On a wooden figure representing a great man, the relatives carved pictures of his many slaves and the heads he had taken. If he was a great hunter, they carved pictures of the elephants, tigers, and other animals he had killed. Some of the wood slabs were taller than a man in order that all the accomplishments of a great warrior and hunter might be shown. That these people had existed was just as sure to me as if I had read about them in a written history by Toynbee or Herodotus.

Around the time of the American Revolution, it was popular in European and American intellectual circles to sneer at the historical record of the Bible, especially the Old Testament. Unbelievers argued that since *only* the Bible mentioned certain names, places, and events of ancient history, the record must be mythical.

But soon biblical names, dates, places, and peoples began

coming alive. Relics had been found, but no one had been able to decipher the strange hieroglyphics (picture language). Then in 1799 a French soldier found a huge basalt slab near Rosetta, Egypt, covered with inscriptions in hieroglyphic, Demotic, and Greek languages. I've seen the stone in the British Museum. By comparing the parallel texts, Jean François Champollion grasped the key to understanding hieroglyphics.

With more discoveries, the ancient civilizations described in the Bible began to be verified. The sites of Babylon, Nineveh, Ur of the Chaldees, and other long-lost cities were uncovered. Creation and flood stories from other cultures were unearthed. The great Code of Hammurabi, which predated the Ten Commandments, was found and translated.

The most critical skeptics stood amazed at the astounding similarities to biblical events.

For example, a Babylonian creation tale reads in part:

> In sin one with another in compact joins.
> The command was established in the garden of God.
> The Ansan-tree they ate, they broke in two.
> Great is their sin. Themselves they exalted.

The Babylonians and other ancients knew life could not have just happened. But in many respects their stories were wildly fanciful. The Babylonians attributed creation to a group of warring deities. The earth, they held, was formed from a leftover carcass on the battlefield.

Most likely, the Babylonians and other cultures simply copied from the biblical account.

Abraham's ancestral city was unearthed. Skeptics had been saying that the stories of the biblical patriarchs were myths, that people in the time claimed for Abraham in the Bible did not even know how to write. Archaeology shattered these charges. The evidence showed Abraham's hometown to have been a thriving metropolis long before the biblical time of the patriarch. Ur had well-laid-out streets and shops. Urites excelled in penmanship, math, geometry, grammar, and the fine arts. They played harps, flutes, trumpets, lyres, drums, and cymbals.

The Hittites were another favorite laughing stock of the skeptics. That the Bible mentioned them over forty times was not sufficient reason to believe they ever existed. Then the archaeologist's spade began turning up Hittite inscriptions. Even the Hittite capital of Hattusas (modern Boghaykoy) was uncovered. By 1900 even the most stubborn unbelievers had to admit that the biblical record was correct. Indeed, the Hittites had once been as powerful as the Egyptians and Assyrians.

The story of Jericho's walls falling down flat at the trumpet blasts of Joshua's soldiers was another source of amusement. Doubters pointed to the existing city of Jericho, which had been reliably dated only to the time of Christ and which revealed no evidence of such a happening in the past.

Then Dr. John Garstang discovered "old" Jericho about a mile north of the Jericho in Jesus' day. Scientific dating established that old Jericho had been destroyed about 1400 B.C., the approximate time of Joshua's victory. Evidence showed the city was surrounded by double walls, connected by beams at the top, on which houses had been built as described in Joshua 2:15. There was also a single gateway to the city as noted in Joshua 2:5–7. The outer wall had toppled backward, down an incline, dragging the inner wall behind. The underlying layer of earth was undisturbed. The walls had not been undermined. The city had been destroyed by fire as reported in Joshua 6:24 and had not been looted before being set afire, supporting Joshua 6:18. Finally, no other city had been built on the site for centuries, which agrees with Joshua 6:26 and 1 Kings 16:34.

Many more witnesses of archaeology to the authenticity of the Old Testament, as well as the New Testament, could be cited. I will mention just one witness concerning the New Testament.

About a century ago, a young English scholar named William Ramsay went to Asia Minor to prove what he had been taught—that Dr. Luke's history as recorded in the Book of Acts was full of errors. After years of painstaking study, Ramsay declared Acts to be completely trustworthy in every historical and geographical detail, and that he himself had become a Christian.

More recently, archaeology has brought forth the testimony of the famous Dead Sea Scrolls and the sensational Ebla Tablets. I will say more about the Scrolls a bit later. Sixteen thousand five hundred tablets and fragments were uncovered at Ebla, Syria, by Italian archaeologists during the last decade. The inscriptions were published in detail in 1981, with the archaeologists crediting the Old Testament with much greater historical accuracy than ever thought possible by secular scholars.

The witness of archaeology has not "proved" everything in the Bible. However, it *has* scientifically verified many, many parts of the biblical record. Furthermore, Dr. Nelson Glueck, one of the greatest archaeologists of the twentieth century, states, "No archaeological discovery has ever controverted a biblical reference."

Fourth is *the witness of science*. Although the Bible is not a textbook on science, it contains hundreds of scientific facts, as up to date as tomorrow's newspaper.

Some 3,000 years before William Harvey proclaimed his theory of the circulation of the blood, the Bible declared, "The life of the flesh is in the blood . . ." (Lev. 17:11). Medical science was a long time accepting the view of Harvey and the Bible. As late as George Washington's time, the draining of blood from the bodies of the seriously ill was still believed to be a curative for every disease. While phlebotomy (bloodletting) is still called for in a few instances, physicians today know that the excessive loss of blood weakens the body.

It was also once commonly thought that the earth was flat. The Flat Earth Society today perpetuates this myth and rejects pictures made from space as propaganda. The Bible agrees with space science. Isaiah 40:22 speaks of the Lord sitting on the circle of the earth. Many ancients also thought the earth was held in place by an under-support. But Job 26:7 declares, "He stretches out the north over empty space, / And hangs the earth on nothing" (NASB).

Job also speaks of how "the morning stars sang together" (Job 38:7). Scoffers once dismissed this as impossible. Now we know there is a beautiful unity and harmony in light and sound. Light properties can have wave motions. If we could hear at the proper frequency, our ears might pick up the melody in the color coming from stars of different temperatures.

Jeremiah declared that "the host [stars] of heaven cannot be numbered" (33:22). The Greek astronomer Hipparchus, who lived hundreds of years after Jeremiah, stated dogmatically that there are only 1,056 stars in the heavens. "I have counted them," he said with assurance. Several centuries later the scientist Ptolemy confirmed Hipparchus's count as correct. Not until A.D. 1610 did Galileo, a Bible-believing Christian, peer through a telescope and proclaim, "There are more stars than we can count." Now we know that billions of stars hang in our Milky Way galaxy alone and that uncounted trillions are suspended in billions upon billions of other galaxies.

No human can explain exactly how the biblical miracles were performed. Astronaut Jack Lousma echoes the belief of many Bible-believing scientists: "Miracles . . . are perfectly possible because God is capable of doing anything, even that which science can't explain."

In many instances, skeptics set out to disprove a biblical miracle and ended up becoming believers. Gilbert West and George Lyttelton, prominent English authors of the eighteenth century, each agreed to write a book exposing the falsity of a New Testament event. West wrote *Observations on the Resurrection*, and Lyttelton penned *Observations on the Conversion of Paul*. They worked independently and when they met, each confessed that he had become a believer in the biblical record.

A few years ago a brash young college student was challenged by his professor to disprove the resurrection of Christ. The result of the search was that the young man became a Christian. Josh McDowell is today one of the foremost defenders of the Christian faith.

"Heaven and earth shall pass away," said Jesus, "but my words shall not pass away" (Matt. 24:35). Only God's Word is unchanging amidst the flood of new information now engulfing us. At Princeton University Dr. Walter Stewart asked several students coming out of a seminar, "How did it go?" "Wonderful," one cracked. "Everything we knew about physics last week isn't true." That will never be said of the Bible.

"But we have only copies and translations of the Bible," I am often reminded. "How can we be sure that the original text is accurate?" I'm always happy to hear that question, for *the witness of the preservation of the text* is another marvelous witness for the greatness of the Bible.

Almost all the Old Testament was written in Hebrew. (Only Ezra 4:8–6:18,7:12–26; Jeremiah 10:11; and Daniel 2:4–7:28 are believed to have been penned in Aramaic.) Biblical Hebrew before the Babylonian exile was written right to left, without vowels, and without spacing between the words or paragraphs. "The Lord is my Shepherd" would appear thus, using English letters and reading right to left: DRHPHSMSDRLHT.

Furthermore, many of the Hebrew consonants looked very much alike, fairly begging for copying mistakes. The R was represented by ר ; DH by ד ; and W by ו . H (ה) and T (ת) appeared similar and so did N (נ) and G (ג). How difficult it must have been to avoid slips in copying on animal skin parchments.

The Hebrew scribes were called *sopherim,* literally meaning "the counters." They deserved this title because they counted every letter of every book of Scripture to make sure that nothing was left out. Then they counted the number of times a particular word appeared in a book and checked each letter that appeared in the middle of each book and in the middle of each major section of the book. The Hebrew Bible was literally copied jot by jot, tittle by tittle, dot by dot.

None of the biblical autographs in Hebrew and Aramaic are believed to have survived because of the scribal practice of destroying deteriorating manuscripts after they were copied. Up until the discovery of the Dead Sea Scrolls, the oldest Hebrew copies dated only to the tenth century of the Christian era, although Greek versions are preserved from a much earlier time. The famous Dead Sea Scrolls were found to contain the texts of many Old Testament books, including a complete copy of Isaiah, written *before* the birth of Christ. Comparison revealed only minute differences between the Scrolls and later copies, and in no case was any major doctrine affected.

Writing skills and language were more advanced by the first century A.D. when the twenty-seven books of the New Testament were written, probably on papyrus paper. These books and letters circulated independently and were passed from church to church, with copies made for further study by the congregation. Because papyrus soon grows brittle with age, the Greek originals are probably lost forever.

The belief that the writings of the apostles and early church leaders were inspired grew until around A.D. 350 when the New Testament Gospels and Epistles that we have today were brought together in a canon. In A.D. 367 the noted theologian Athanasius declared: "In these alone is the teaching of godliness heralded. Let no one add to these. Let nothing be taken away." The New Testament books were added to the thirty-nine Old Testament books, already accepted by Jews and Christians as inspired, to make the Bible as we have it today.

Not considering the Old Testament, over 24,000 Greek and Latin manuscripts of all or part of the New Testament have been preserved. The oldest portion, called the Rylands Papyrus, (John 18:31–33,37,38) dates to around A.D. 150, less than fifty years after the death of the apostle John. The Bodmer manuscript, containing Luke 3–24, dates to about A.D. 200. More complete New Testament manuscripts are preserved from the third and fourth centuries.

No other ancient book has as much manuscript evidence as the Bible. Only a single manuscript preserves the famous history written by the Roman writer Tacitus, for example. Only a handful of copies exist of the writings of such scholars as Homer, Cicero, Virgil, and Sophocles.

The agreement of the New Testament manuscripts, which come from all parts of the Greek and Roman world, is amazing. Dr. A. T. Robertson, the foremost biblical Greek scholar of the twentieth century, found notable variances in only one one-thousandth of the New Testament texts, with none of the differences being of any real significance.

The scholar Jerome first translated the entire Bible. His Latin Vulgate appeared in A.D. 405 and became the authorized Catholic version. Around 1250, Cardinal Hugo divided the books of the Bible into chapters. Verse divisions were not made until 1551 by Robert Stephanus.

John Wycliffe first translated the Bible into English. Each Wycliffe Bible took about ten months to copy by hand and cost $200. Few could afford to buy one. Many paid just to hear Scripture read for one hour in their native English. Some copies were sold page by page.

More translations kept appearing, but not until after the development of printing presses with movable type did the Bible attain mass circulation. The first printed Bible came off Johann Gutenberg's press around 1450. One copy of Gutenberg's Bible is now in the United States Library of Congress and is valued at over one million dollars.

Although printing is believed to have been invented by the Chinese centuries earlier, it was in Europe that the new technology caught on. More books appeared in the last half of the fifteenth century than in all previous human history. Almost half were on biblical themes, with more than 150 editions of the Bible published. "Printing," said Martin Luther, "is God's latest and best work to spread the true religion through the world."

The march of the Bible was just beginning. One edition after another appeared in England. In the haste to satisfy the thirst of the masses, some were a little less than perfect. Psalm 119:161 read in one translation: "Printers have persecuted me without a cause." Another difficulty was the rapid changing of definitions and spellings. The Taverner Bible had a messenger reporting to King David during a battle: "I saw a great hurlee burlee" (2 Sam. 18:29).

Every new edition and translation brought improvement. Most notable was the Bible commissioned by King James I in 1611. King James hoped that a new Bible would heal divisions within the English church. The translators were the greatest biblical scholars of that day. They produced the most popular version of the Bible for all time.

Many more versions and translations of the Bible have appeared since the King James. George Cowan, a former president of the Wycliffe Bible Translators, notes that the Bible has been translated into over 1700 languages during the past 175 years, with 500 coming in the past quarter century. Currently, a portion of the Scripture is appearing in a new language on the average of one every fourteen days. Wycliffe Bible Translators are now working in over 600 additional languages, and the United Bible Societies are involved in translation projects in more than 500 languages around the world.

How marvelous is the faithful preservation of the text of the Scripture!

A sixth witness to the wonder of the Bible is *the Bible's triumph over its enemies*. No book has incurred so much opposition from unkind kings and infidels, corrupt churchmen and unbelieving scholars, and from Fascist and Communist governments. From ancient times to the present, mobs have burned the Bible in public squares and soldiers have ransacked homes to find and destroy the Book of the Ages. All have proved futile. Indeed, the Bible has multiplied with every assault on it.

King Manasseh of Judah came to the throne of Judah in 687 B.C. when he was only twelve years old. He made paganism the state religion and even had children sacrificed to the god Molech. The Word of God disappeared during his sinful reign. Yet twenty years after Manasseh's death, his grandson, Josiah, found the lost Book of the Law in the temple and called for public reading and observance. A powerful religious revival swept the land.

Jehoiakim, another evil king of Judah, tried and failed to destroy the Word of God about 600 B.C. Angered at the written prophecy of Jeremiah, he cut up the book and threw it into the fire. But the Word remained and at God's command was rewritten and enlarged.

Some 500 years later the Syrian despot, Antiochus Epiphanes seized control of the land of the Jews. He plundered the sacred temple, sacrificed swine on the altar, and appointed inspectors to ferret out every copy of Scripture in the land. Anyone found possessing a copy of the Old Testament was killed on the spot.

The massacres, sacrilege, and Bible burnings by Antiochus ignited a revolution. The patriotic Maccabees raised a guerilla army and defeated the foreign invaders. Three years after ordering the Hebrew Scripture destroyed, Antiochus died in humiliation. The temple was repaired, worship reinstituted, and Scripture again taught publicly.

The Romans (in control of Palestine when Jesus was born) permitted the Jews to read and teach the Bible. They ignored the Christian movement for a while, believing it only a sect of the Jews. But as Christians grew in number and refused to acknowledge Caesar as divine, the Romans became alarmed. The emperors of Rome executed tens of thousands of Christians and confiscated their Bibles.

Perhaps the worst persecutor was Emperor Diocletian. In A.D. 303 he determined to destroy Christianity and the Bible. Diocletian's army slaughtered untold numbers of believers during a two-year blood bath, and the emperor erected a monument over the ashes of a Bible, with the inscription, *Extincto nomine Christianorum*—"Extinct is the Name of Christians!"

Less than twenty years later a new ruler, Emperor Constantine, professed faith in Christ himself and asked every person in the Empire to read the Bible!

During the Dark Ages the Bible was kept from the people by misguided church leaders. For the most part, the sacred Book was preserved only in monasteries and not considered safe for ordinary people to read. But the Bible could not be kept bound. The Word burst forth as a flood with the Reformation and the advance of printing.

As revival and renewal spread across Europe, some state monarchs continued to oppose the Bible. "Bloody" Queen Mary made Bible printing and distribution a capital offense. Benjamin Franklin recalled that his great-great-grandfather had fastened a Bible under a stool. When he wanted to read to his family, he simply turned the stool upside-down as one of the children stood watch for Bloody Mary's soldiers.

Mary's five-year reign of terror ended with her death in 1558. Her half-sister Elizabeth took the crown and reversed the policy of hatred for the Bible. Elizabeth ordered a Bible placed in every court and called Scripture "the jewel I love best." Ninety editions of the Geneva Bible were published during her long reign, plus forty editions of other versions.

The eighteenth century brought attacks on the Bible from French rationalists. Ernest Renan attacked biblical miracles and ridiculed the idea that Jesus was divine. However, before his death Renan declared, "O man of Galilee, Thou hast conquered. Henceforth no man shall distinguish between Thee and God!"

Most outspoken was François Voltaire who boasted, "One hundred years from my day there will not be a Bible in the earth except one that is looked upon by an antiquarian curiosity-seeker."

Two hundred years later a first edition of Voltaire's writing sold in Paris for eleven cents. That same day the British Government paid Soviet Russia $500,000 for the famous New Testament manuscript, Codex Sinaiticus, which had been found in an old monastery near Mount Sinai.

During the nineteenth century destructive higher criticism undermined the Bible in German universities and seminaries. This weakened the German church and aided Hitler's rise to power and Nazi persecution of Jews. Yet the Nazis could not stamp out the Bible. A symbol of its continuing power was demonstrated in the last request of

German soldiers, surrounded by counterattacking Soviet troops in Stalingrad. Their last wireless message pleaded, "Send us Bibles." German planes flew over enemy lines and dropped precious copies of the Word of God.

Emperor Hirohito of Japan had as his goal the wiping out of the Bible and Christianity and establishing Shintoism as the great world religion. Both Hitler and Hirohito went down in defeat, Hitler probably dying by his own hand and Hirohito admitting to his people that he was not divine. Germany once again became a base for sending missionaries and Bibles around the world. And in Japan, Captain Mitsuo Fuchida, the man who led the Japanese attack on Pearl Harbor, was converted and became a distributor of Bibles.

The witness of the Bible's triumph over its enemies continues. The death camps of the Soviet Union have been unable to destroy the Bible and faith. Even while many believers suffer in Soviet concentration camps, the Word of God is copied and passed from hand to hand in the Soviet Union and other Communist countries.

Now we are finding that, after years of suppression, the Bible has remained alive in China. During the radical Cultural Revolution, almost all Chinese churches were closed, religious leaders attacked and imprisoned, and their Bibles burned. Still the Christians met in small house-churches to share testimonies and prayer and read or quote from memory precious passages from God's Word. They tore the Bible into portions so they could share it with others. One would copy a few pages, return it, then receive another. Some learned passages by heart and went from group to group dictating Scripture to fellow believers who wrote it down.

One of the most listened-to radio programs now being beamed into mainland China is called "The Most Popular Book in English." The program is simply Bible readings in English and Chinese. Scores of letters have come to the Far

East Broadcasting Company expressing thanks for the Bible.

The Book of the Ages endures because it is the Book that stands. Barring the return of our Lord, I expect the Bible to be the Book of books a hundred years, yea, a thousand years from now.

Allow me one more illustration of this truth. I was only a boy in a mission school, far back in the Indian jungle, when the New York World's Fair was held in 1939. I did not even know the great event was going on. I certainly did not know that a time capsule of items was buried at the fair, not to be dug up for 5,000 years when archaeologists of another time could learn about the twentieth century.

Only one full-size book was stuffed into the capsule—the Bible. When asked why the Bible had been chosen, an official said: "The Holy Bible, of all books familiar to us today, will most likely survive through the ages. Therefore, the Bible that we placed in the time capsule will be a sort of connecting link between past, present, and future."

The Bible, above all books, is the Book that stands.

Chapter 3

The Book for Humanity

NEVER HAD I seen so many books in one place. I walked softly, reverently beside the wall of books in the library of the Jorhat mission high school. I was so impressed. There were probably no more than 500 or 600 volumes, yet at sixteen I thought they must contain all the wisdom of the world. If the librarian would have permitted, I would have slept and taken all my meals beside those books.

At that time I had no idea of the vast number of books in the world. I had never heard of the Library of Congress, which now houses over twelve million books and pamphlets in two buildings covering thirty-six acres of floor space. Two copies of every new book published and copyrighted in the United States have been filed there since 1870. This book will be among some 40,000 which will be cataloged and shelved in the Library of Congress this year.

Forty thousand *new* books are published in one year in the United States alone! Books on every conceivable subject, from asteroids to zephyrs. The author of Ecclesiastes was right. ". . . of making many books there is no end . . ." (12:12).

Only about one in 200 among the new books will make any best seller list. Only one of ten best sellers will remain in that category for as long as ten weeks. Only one-half of one percent of all books published will last seven years. Go to the library and look at the list of best sellers in *Time* or *Publisher's Weekly* for a year ago. Open any page of *Books in Print* a year ago and read the names of the first one hundred titles. See how few, if any, you remember.

Writer Alice Payne Hackett lists all the best sellers in the United States for the period 1895–1965. She found that only 633 titles in both hard cover and paperback had sold over a million copies. *The Pocket Book of Baby and Child Care* by Dr. Benjamin Spock tops her list, selling over 19 million copies.

Although Ms. Hackett does not include the Bible, she says:

> Any discussion of such a list must start with the Bible. The general public probably asks more questions of libraries and trade specialists about the Bible than about any other book. The most familiar question is, "Is the Bible *the* best seller?" The answer is unequivocally in the affirmative.★

Horace Shipp's *Books That Moved the World* includes as the top ten:
1. *The Bible*
2. *The Republic,* Plato
3. *The City of God,* St. Augustine
4. *The Koran*
5. *The Divine Comedy,* Dante
6. *Plays,* Shakespeare
7. *Pilgrim's Progress,* Bunyan
8. *Areopagitica,* Milton

★Alice Payne Hackett, *70 years of Best Sellers, 1875–1965* (New York: R. B. Bowker, 1967).

  9. *The Origin of Species,* Darwin
  10. *Das Kapital,* Marx*

Heading the list is the Bible. Four of the remaining nine are directly lated to the Bible. *The City of God* is a defense and explanation of Christianity. *The Koran* is packed with historical material from the Bible, but with many significant differences. *The Divine Comedy* is a medieval interpretation of the Bible. *Pilgrim's Progress* is a biblical allegory.

Shakespeare's *Plays* are infused with biblical ideas. Milton's *Areopagitica* builds a brilliant defense of freedom of the press upon biblical concepts. Milton also penned the Bible-centered classics, *Paradise Lost* and *Paradise Regained.*

The three other members of Shipp's top ten deal with themes prominent in the Bible. The *Republic* presents Plato's ideal society; the Bible proclaims the kingdom of God. Darwin deals with origins; the Bible declares, "In the beginning God created . . ." (Gen. 1:1). Marx discusses the nature of history and the purpose of man in *Das Kapital;* the Bible says history is under the sovereignty of God and man was made to glorify God.

The Bible also heads James Bennett's list of fifty *Great Classics.* Bennett calls the Bible a fount of great literature which "brought to perfection the short story" and "originated" the literary style of free verse.

Why, among the myriads of books published, is the Bible the all-time best seller and most influential among all books? The primary reason, I believe, is that the Bible is the Book most able to meet man's deepest needs. It is, above all books, the *Book* for humanity.

Marketing experts say modern publishing has moved

---

*Cited by Robert B. Downs, *Books That Changed the World* (Chicago: American Library Association, 1977), p. 10.

sharply towards specialization. Most nonfiction books are written, edited, and promoted with special interest groups in mind. Have you noticed all the diet books in the bookstores recently? Books on running and physical exercise? Books advising us how to make financial ends meet? Books about the dangers of nuclear warfare? Books about the single life? Books telling us how to get along in the family and improve our marriage? Each is addressed to a special need and readership.

Not *everybody* is interested in dieting or in help for living alone. But enough people are interested to justify publishing books in these areas. The Bible, however, is a *universal* book, with something for everyone. Almost every person asks these questions: Why am I here? What is the ultimate meaning of life? Is there life after death? How can I satisfy the deepest longings of my heart? How can I be rid of the burden of guilt? How can I learn to love others? How can I find happiness in my family? Such questions cannot be answered by science or philosophy. Only the Bible gives fully satisfactory—and eternally significant—answers.

When translated into a mother tongue, the Bible is as relevant and life-changing for the Aucas of the rain forests of eastern Ecuador as it is for the Nafanra people of Ghana, the Tinputz tribe of Papua New Guinea, the stockbrokers of Wall Street, the street cleaners of Calcutta, and the peasants of the People's Republic of China.

My good friend Paul Krishna searched for answers to the great questions of life. Raised a Hindu, he prayed daily with his brothers and sisters at a little shrine. But in college he lost confidence in his religion and became enamored with Marxism.

After becoming disenchanted with Communist ideas, he sought satisfaction in law practice. When success in a profession did not fill the vacuum, he went back for a Ph.D., then took a post as head of the Department of Oriental

Studies at University College in Durban, South Africa. He enjoyed the life of a teacher-scholar for a while, then the old emptiness returned. Surely there must be something more, he thought.

One morning when driving to the university he picked up a laborer hitch-hiking to his job. The man shared his Christian faith. Paul envied the man's peace and contentment. Later three students from a nearby Bible college stopped at Paul's house and left a New Testament.

"A verse from Matthew startled and sent an electric thrill through me," Paul recalls. "I read these magnificent words from God: 'Come unto me, all ye that labor and are heavy laden, and I will give you rest' " (11:28).

Paul couldn't get enough of the Bible. Often he read until the early hours of the morning. He asked for Christian baptism and two days later boarded a plane to come to the United States. This lawyer and distinguished professor entered Trinity Evangelical Divinity School to prepare for a new career of preaching and teaching the Word of God. Every time I see Paul, I marvel at the glow on his face.

I was sharing Paul Krishna's story with a good friend when he told me about a Russian seminary classmate of his who had found spiritual rest and purpose for living from the same Bible verse.

Nikolai Alexandrenko, he said, was a student in a Russian military academy when World War II erupted. Commissioned an officer in the paratroops at nineteen, Nikolai was made commander of a company and dropped into the front lines near the Dnieper River where the Germans were advancing toward Moscow.

The company was moving against a nest of German riflemen when German tanks roared down upon them. Suddenly Nikolai felt a sharp pain in his left leg. He looked and saw blood and knew he was hit. The standing order to Russian officers was "suicide before capture." Nikolai started to swing the barrel of his gun toward his temple. He hesistated, then threw the gun away and hopped toward an approaching Nazi tank, hands high in surrender.

The Germans shoved him into a railroad cattle car with nineteen other captured soldiers. As the train was moving out, Russian planes swooped in and bombed their own soldiers. Only Nikolai and one other survived.

Nikolai was put in a prison camp in Munich. His wounds went untreated and he almost starved on a diet of "grass soup." Hundreds of his fellow prisoners died from hunger.

In 1945 the war ended, and he was told he could return home. "If I go back, they'll send me to Siberia for surrendering," he pleaded. "Let me stay in Germany."

His new home was a displaced persons camp. As month after weary month passed, questions came for which atheism had no answer. "Why was my life spared during the war? Why did I survive in the prison camp when so many others died of starvation?"

One morning, while in a despondent frame of mind, Nikolai noticed the fire had gone out in the barracks' stove. Apparently someone had stuffed the door full with waste paper, cutting off the oxygen. He tossed a lighted match into the rubbish. When the flame failed to catch, he bent over to shove the trash back into the stove. That's when he noticed two verses from the New Testament on a torn, dirty slip of paper: "Come unto me, all ye that labor and are heavy laden, and I will give you rest. . . . Behold, I stand at the door, and knock: if any man hear my voice, and open the door, I will come in to him" (Matt. 11:28; Rev. 3:20).

The paper said the words were from Jesus Christ, whom Nikolai had been told in school was only a character from Christian mythology. "What if He is the Son of God?" the weary refugee asked. "Could He give me rest?"

"Oh, God, if You exist, help me," Nikolai cried. "If Christ truly be Your Son, give me rest. Show me the way."

Warm tears trickled down his cheeks. He had not cried since he was a child—not even when his mother died, not on the battlefield, not when tortured by hunger pangs in the prison camp. Now as he wiped away the tears, a strange warmth and tender calmness enveloped his heart.

A few days later he ran into an old friend from the Russian army. The friend said he had also become a Christian and offered to get Nikolai a Bible.

Nikolai read the Bible through in a month. He was baptized and began preaching to Russian refugees. Many responded to the biblical messages from the former atheist.

Now here—as my friend related it and as Paul Harvey would say—is "the rest of the story." Within ten years Nikolai earned a doctor of theology degree and was teaching the Bible in a Christian college. He is still doing so today.

World War II, from which Nikolai Alexandrenko is only one of millions of refugees, was supposed to end all wars. It didn't. The official count of regional wars since now stands at 130. That doesn't include conflicts that have raged inside nations so long they now are taken for granted. Perhaps most agonizing has been the conflict in the Middle East. Fighting now surges in Lebanon, where sixty thousand lives have been taken since 1976. Iran and Iraq continue locked in bloody combat. An estimated six to ten thousand people died in Syria this year in the suppression of an internal revolt. Riots and killings continue on the West Bank of the Jordan, which has not known peace for almost thirty-five years.

What can be done about the hatreds and animosities that keep bursting forth in bloody wars? Is there any healing for bitterness between Arabs and Jews?

My Arab friend Anis Shorrosh says he found the solution in the Bible. Anis calls himself a member of the new PLO— Palestinians Loving Others. But he was "as hateful as a man could be, before he found in the Bible the way to love."

One winter afternoon in Chicago, Anis shared his gripping story. He was a lad of fifteen in Nazareth, the hometown of Jesus, when Israel proclaimed itself a state and fighting broke out with the Arabs. Anis's father and uncle were killed in that war. He fled with his mother, brother, and sister across the Jordan River.

"Ro, you can't imagine how revengeful I felt. Our family had to live in just one room. I could not get a job or go to school. My only identity was a ration card issued by the United Nations, allowing me nine cents worth of food each day.

"Oh, how I hated. I hated the British because they had exploited my people and then abandoned us to the Jews. I hated the Jordanians and Syrians for not coming to our aid. I hated the Jews for killing my loved ones and forcing my family to flee. If I could have gotten a gun, I would have gone back and killed every Jew in sight until they killed me."

After months of brooding and despair, Anis ran out into the desert and lay down on the rocky ground, waiting to die. "I thought if I didn't starve to death, the heat would kill me. Or if not that, wild animals or a poisonous snake would end my miserable life.

"As I lay there in the desert, boyhood memories flashed before me. I thought of my selfish life. I remembered the time when I had piled stones on the railroad track in Haifa, almost causing the train to wreck and endangering hundreds of people. Never had I felt so wretched."

Morning came and the sun and dryness sucked at his body moisture. His mouth became parched, his lips split, and he became delirious from fever. By afternoon his vision was blurred. By sunset he was incoherent, alternately laughing and crying, mocking himself.

"Ro, I thought this is what hell must be like. I knew if there was such a place, I was a good candidate. Not wanting to take that chance, I got up and stumbled home to Mother. She welcomed me with open arms."

The next morning was Easter. Anis spent the day reading his mother's Bible.

"I read for three days," Anis recalled. "Finally, I stopped where Jesus said, in the Sermon on the Mount, 'Seek ye first the kingdom of God, and his righteousness; and all these things shall be added unto you' [Matt. 6:33]. I knew God was real and that if my life was ever to change I would have to put Him first. I knelt beside my sleeping mat and gave Him the rest of my life."

When Anis accepted the promise of Christ, things began to happen. He got a job. Missionaries arranged for him to attend college in the United States. Today, Dr. Anis Shorrosh is a worldwide evangelist, proclaiming the love of God to Arabs, Jews, and thousands of others around the world.

Anis makes his headquarters in the United States, but twice a year he makes a trip back to his shattered homeland. On one occasion he was accompanied by a choir from a church in Florida.

The choir was invited to sing for wounded Israeli soldiers before television cameras. After the program, Anis recalled for the soldiers the killing of his loved ones by Israelis and the loss of his home in Nazareth. "I hated Jews with all the intensity of my being for what had been done to my family," he said. "But now, I want to tell you that I love you because of Jesus."

Another time he was escorting a group of Christian pilgrims to Nazareth. As they neared the hometown of Jesus, the tour guide recalled to the Arab at his side that he had been commander of the tank company that had taken Nazareth in the 1948 war. Anis listened, struggling to control his emotions. When the Israeli finished, Anis looked at him and said, "I am a native of Nazareth. My father and uncle were killed there, probably by your men. By all the traditions of my people, I ought to kill you and take revenge. I cannot, I can only say, 'I love you,' because of my Savior, Jesus of Nazareth. May I show you what the Bible says about His love?"

When I think of how the Bible can change hatred into love, fill emptiness with meaning, and turn sadness into joy, a talented young Italian professor comes to mind. As a young man he broke his mother's heart. Caring not for virtue, he fathered an illegitimate son and lived with the mother out of wedlock. Then he swung to the opposite extreme and joined a cult that taught that all sexual desire is evil.

After twelve years, he became disillusioned with the cult's leader and went to Rome seeking answers. He dabbled in Greek philosophy. He went to hear a renowned Christian preacher who convinced him that the Bible was the Word of God. He yearned to become a Christian and live a holy life but couldn't control his sinful passions.

One July day, when at his wit's end, he cried to God for deliverance. That moment he heard a child chanting, "*Tolle lege! Tolle lege!* Take and read! Take and read!"

He opened the Bible to the Book of Romans and his eyes fell upon: "not in rioting and drunkenness, not in chambering and wantonness, not in strife and envying. But put ye on the Lord Jesus Christ, and make not provision for the flesh, to fulfill the lusts thereof" (13:13,14).

"I have put on Christ!" he shouted to a friend. "My heart is glowing with peace."

This gifted man of the fourth century became the greatest Christian writer since the apostle Paul. Aurelius Augustine wrote more than seventy books, two of which, *City of God* and *Confessions,* still rank among the world's greatest literature.

St. Augustine expressed the deepest longing of every man's heart when he wrote: "Thou hast made us for Thyself, O Lord, and our souls will never rest until they find rest in Thee." The great French mathematician, Blaise Pascal declared, "There is a God-shaped vacuum in the heart of every man which only God can fill through His Son, Jesus Christ."

Only the Bible, among the books held sacred in the history of mankind, tells us how to fill that vacuum. Only the Bible tells us that we are made in the image and likeness of God (Gen. 1:27). Though we have marred that image by sin, only the Bible tells us how to find cleansing and become a new creation in Christ.

Nothing else can quench this thirst. H. G. Wells, famed historian and philosopher who rejected the Bible as inspired truth, lamented at the age of sixty-one, "I have no peace. All life is at the end of its tether." And England's great poet Lord Byron, who disdained Christian morality and rejected the Bible as a life guide, wrote, "My days are in the yellow leaf, the flowers and fruits of life are gone, the worm and the canker and the grief are mine alone."

King David cried in the wilderness: "O God, thou art my God; early will I seek thee: my soul thirsteth for thee, my flesh longeth for thee in a dry and thirsty land . . ." (Ps. 63:1). Only the Bible tells how this thirst can be satisfied. Said Jesus to the woman at the well: "Whoever drinks of the water [believes in me] that I shall give him shall never thirst; but the water that I shall give him shall become in him a well of water springing up to eternal life" (John 4:14 NASB).

Young Francis Bernardone discovered this living water and became one of the most heroic figures of history. As a young man, Francis was a playboy in Italy's Tiber Valley. Son of a wealthy cloth merchant from the town of Assisi, Francis spent his days and nights in revelry. Then war broke out and Francis was captured. After a stay in prison and a grave illness, Francis began seeking a deeper meaning in life.

Francis found the secret of life in the Bible. He vowed to serve Christ for the rest of his life, but he did not know what he was to do until he read these words from the Bible:

> As ye go, preach, saying, The kingdom of heaven is at hand. Heal the sick, cleanse the lepers, raise the dead, cast out devils: freely ye have received, freely give. Provide neither gold, nor silver, nor brass in your purses, nor scrip for your journey, neither two coats, neither shoes, nor yet staves: for the workman is worthy of his meat (Matt. 10:7–10).

"From this time on, my life will be one of Gospel poverty," Francis declared. Leaving his wealth behind, Francis set out with eleven equally committed companions for a humble ministry of preaching and ministering to the sick and needy. The Franciscans, as they came to be called, left a greater mark for good on medieval Europe than many kings and popes. The great Protestant church historian Philip Schaff wrote of their noble leader, "Few men of history have made so profound an impression as Francis of Assisi."

The Bible is the Book for humanity at every stage of life, but it is particularly meaningful when life seems most fragile. Communists overran part of Korea, murdering and imprisoning Christians; a pastor's wife fled with her baby, a bag of rice, and her precious Bible. Knowing that she might be killed if caught with the Bible, she was tempted to leave it behind, but she tucked it in her bosom and went on. Later she hid the Book of books in a cave. Each day at sunset she crept cautiously to the cave to read words that "made my heart leap!"

When the Communists came closer, she fled further south. Finding shelter in a village, she hid the Bible under a stone floor and sheltered the baby in a foxhole. When the fighting finally stopped, she still had her baby and her Bible.

Eddie Rickenbacker is one of the great war heroes of World War II. Rickenbacker and seven other American airmen were forced down in the Pacific about six hundred miles north of Samoa. Day after fear-filled day they drifted on a rubber raft. Their food and water ran out. They were tortured by hunger and thirst. High waves tossed them about. Hungry sharks circled, waiting for the kill. Some men in the group became delirious. But Rickenbacker never lost hope. His solace was a Bible from which he gathered strength. When they were rescued after twenty-four days on the water, Rickenbacker said the Bible had saved them.

My friend Edward Lacaba grew up on the remote island of Cebu in the Philippines. In his teens he lost faith in the idol-worshiping religion of his family. The death of a beloved brother caused great anguish. His father's business failure and poor grades in school dropped him deeper into the pit of despair. When the Japanese invaded, he fled with his family to a mountain hideaway. There he came across a tiny book, hidden in a dry nook by a departed American soldier. The book was olive drab in color, one of the millions issued to soldiers by the U.S. government.

In the Gospels Edward saw "a caring Man, a Man of love and righteousness, a Man so real and near that when I came to John 5:24 it was as though Jesus Himself was there and spoke to me: 'Verily, verily, I say unto you, He that heareth my word, and believeth on him that sent me, hath everlasting life. . . .'

"The impact of the words, 'hath everlasting life,' so overwhelmed me that it became the moment of my rebirth," he testifies. "It ushered me into the world of reality. Before, there had been only darkness. Now I discovered Christ's world of light, life, and meaning."

He shared this good news with his parents, brothers, and friends. Many of them believed. Edward Lacaba is today a leading Christian in the Philippines, who "marvels" at the "genuine miracle which began when God's Word entered my life and I received His Son."

The Bible is a precious treasure when one is stripped of family, possessions, job and freedom, and left with no human resources to fall back on.

I was preaching the gospel among the tribal people of my native northeast India when news came that the American intelligence-gathering ship, the Pueblo, had been taken over by North Korea. The capture created a worldwide furor, with many fearing that war might break out between the United States and the North Korean Communist government. After long and delicate negotiations the crew of eighty-two was released after almost a year of captivity. It was then that we learned how the Bible had sustained the eighty-two crewmen during the months of harassment and beatings by their captors.

They didn't have an actual Bible, for their personal effects were taken away. The "Pueblo Bible," as it was called, grew as crew members wrote down verses from memory on toilet paper. They recalled the Twenty-Third Psalm, parts of the Sermon on the Mount, John 3:16, and about twenty other passages. Two special verses of comfort were: "Thou wilt keep him in perfect peace, whose mind is stayed on thee: because he trusteth in thee," and, "Casting all your care upon him; for he careth for you" (Is. 26:3; 1 Pet. 5:7).

"The Bible sustained us and kept us alive," reported Lieutenant Commander Stephen Harris, leader of the intelligence operatives. "My own faith actually became stronger by trusting in the promises of Scripture, even though I never knew for certain whether I would live from one day to the next."

Returning POW's from North Vietnamese prison camps gave the same testimony. Like the Pueblo crew, the Vietnam prisoners compiled their own "Bible" from memory. Favorite passages were the Twenty-Third Psalm, the Beatitudes, Romans 12, and 1 Corinthians 13.

Chaplain Alex Aronis interviewed and counseled many of these prisoners when they were flown to the Philippines from the dread Hanoi prisons. "The key to their survival and mental and emotional health," Chaplain Aronis notes, "was a deep abiding and growing relationship with God." Bible verses remembered from days gone by kept them strong.

Similar stories continue to come of the Bible's sustaining power for prisoners. Just the other day I read the testimony of Wilson Chen in *Christianity Today*. Mr. Chen, a South Vietnamese army officer, was sent to a "reeducation" camp after the Communists took over South Vietnam. For five years he was forced to do excruciatingly hard labor and eat rats, locusts, lizards, frogs, snakes, and other living things just to stay alive. After work, he had to suffer through painful brainwashing sessions. To make his situation worse, he received news while in the camps that his brother had died and that his fiancée had married and fled the country.

Fortunately, Mr. Chen had several small Bibles in Chinese, Vietnamese, and English which he kept hidden in holes around the camp. When the guards were not around, he and his friends took turns reading and encouraging one another. "It was hope in the Lord Jesus that kept me alive," Mr. Chen wrote. "I fed this hope by reading the Scriptures."

Christian leaders of all denominations agree that the Bible is the most important book in the world. In the Philippines, where we mailed 300,000 Bibles from 1978–81 to everyone in the telephone directories, Cardinal Sin of the Roman Catholic church declares:

> Through reading the Bible we learn what God wants us to do. If we really want a new society where honesty and love

for one another exists, then we should begin with the individual . . . [and] conversion. . . . When you are converted you listen to God's Word through reading the Bible and you would like to execute in your personal life what God wants you to do.

The Bible is a very old Book, but it is as up-to-date as tomorrow's newspapers. Not only is it a balm in time of crisis, it is a guide for true success in life. Marion Wade, the founder and long-term chairman of the board of the Service-Master Company, discovered this early in life. Until his death a few years ago, Mr. Wade was one of the finest citizens and best supporters of Christian causes in the Wheaton, Illinois, area. Mr. Wade recalled: "I was especially drawn to Joshua 1:8, which says, 'This book of the law shall not depart out of thy mouth; but thou shalt meditate therein day and night, that thou mayest observe to do according to all that is written therein: for then thou shalt make thy way prosperous, and then thou shalt have good success.' Later I found that this is the only place in the Bible where the word 'success' appears. The truth hit me that I could only succeed with God, my fellow man, and myself by living according to the Bible."

Marion Wade was very active in the Christian Businessmen's Committee which once had offices not far from our headquarters. Many other vocational fellowships meet regularly for Christian companionship and the study of God's Word.

The Music City Christian Fellowship gathers every Thursday at noon in Nashville. Singers, song writers, and other professionals in the music business attend. Marijohn Wilkins is one of their leaders. As a songwriter Marijohn made it big in Nashville, but she found that fame and success did not satisfy. After several personal tragedies, she saw no hope for living. Twice she tried to kill herself. Then she turned to the Bible, which she had loved in her childhood back in Texas. In God's Word she found joy and purpose for living. While wondering how she could be faithful to the commands of God's Word, a prayer came to her mind. "Lord, help me live for you one day at a time." The prayer became the most popular gospel song in history, "One Day at a Time."

The headquarters of the Christian Legal Society is not far from our office. As you might guess, this is a fellowship of lawyers and law students from all Christian denominations. Groups meet regularly across the country to study the Bible and find Scriptural applications to their profession. The Christian Legal Society sponsors the Christian Conciliation Service, which attempts to provide healing and reconciliation to Christian individuals and groups in dispute, before they go to court. The Christian lawyers help disputants find God's way for settling conflicts as outlined in Matthew 18 and 1 Corinthians 6.

The Christian Medical Society is for doctors and medical students. One of their leaders is Dr. C. Everett Koop, Surgeon General of the United States. Bible-believing nurses enjoy the Nurses Christian Fellowship. Athletes find direction for life in Bible study through the Fellowship of Christian Athletes and similar groups. I've been told that every major league baseball and professional club in the United States and Canada has a team chapel where Jesus Christ and His Word are proclaimed. There is a Fellowship of Christian Companies for believers in the corporate business world. In Washington, D.C., the Fellowship Foundation and the Christian Embassy ministers to believers in the diplomatic corps from many countries and to government officials. There are Bible study and prayer groups in the Senate and House of Representatives, the State Department, and many other federal agencies. There is a fellowship for pilots, flight attendants, mechanics, and others employed by commercial airlines. There is even an organization called Cops for Christ.

Bible study groups thrive on practically every college campus in America under the sponsorship of Campus Crusade, Bible Study Fellowship, Christian Women's Club, InterVarsity Christian Fellowship, The Navigators, and other Bible-believing organizations. Hundreds of Campus Life Bible clubs are attended by high schoolers. Converted prisoners meet for prayer and Bible study.

Recently the Prison Fellowship, headed by converted Watergate figure Charles Colson, held a Bible study seminar for fifteen men on Death Row at the Holman Correctional Institution in Alabama—the first time condemned prisoners were ever permitted to congregate in groups larger than three or four. The condemned men asked such questions as, "How can I be sure I will go to heaven after what I've done?" The Bible provided the answer.

This is only in America. Countless other groups, besides the tens of thousands of churches and Sunday schools, meet all over the world to mine rich nuggets from God's Word. In England, for example, there is the Christian Lawyer's Fellowship. In some lands believers must meet in secret to study the Bible, knowing that if discovered they may be arrested and sent to prison.

The depth of this marvelous Book, which appeals to all humanity, can never be fully tapped. After several days of reading the Bible, a Chinese scholar who had been engaged by the American Bible Society to help with a translation project, concluded: "The One who made that Book made me, for it tells me things about myself that no one else knows, and some things that *I* did not even know."

President Woodrow Wilson observed: "Every time you open the Bible, some old text that you have read a score of times suddenly beams with new meaning." Poet Samuel Coleridge reflected: "In the Bible there is more that finds

me than I have experienced in all other books put together."
Dr. Charles Malik, former President of the United Nations
General Assembly, believes: "The Bible is the source of
every good thought and impulse that I have."

Truly the Bible is the Book for humanity, the Book for
every man of every race, culture, and nation to live and die
by. It speaks to men and women, young and old, educated
and uneducated, factory workers and millionaires, to those
of every class and every vocation. They find it fresh every
day, a precious guide for life, a light along the dark paths,
and a sure anchor in stormy weather.

It is the Book of life for all humanity. When Sir Walter
Scott lay dying, he called for "the Book." When asked,
"What book?" the great man of letters replied, "There is
only one Book for this time, the Bible."

It is the Book that abides, for Jesus said, "Heaven and
earth shall pass away, but my words shall not pass away"
(Matt. 24:35).

Chapter 4

The Book
That Shapes
History

"GOOD MORNING, MARY, did you sleep well?" I greeted my lovely sixteen-year-old daughter. "And, John, please have a friend pick you up for college this morning. Your mother and I will need both cars." Then I stopped and thought: "Every time I speak the name of one of my children, I echo the influence of the Bible. Mawii and I gave biblical names to our children—Mary, John, and Paul (who is in graduate school at the University of Illinois)—because of what the Bible means to us. In this we are not unusual. Millions of other parents have given biblical names to their offspring, in every nation where the Bible has gone. Think of all the English "Johns," the German "Johanns," and the Spanish "Juans."

I looked at the calendar and saw again the influence of the Bible. Even Communist nations are forced to date the years from the birth of Christ: A.D., meaning *Anno Domini*—in the year of our Lord, or B.C.—before Christ.

I looked out the window and saw children boarding a yellow school bus, and I saw more influence of the Bible. Universal, free public education is a result of the Protestant

Reformation, which exploded in Europe as the Bible was translated into the vernaculars of the people.

The other day I visited a friend in a hospital. Still again the power of the Bible came to mind. Hospitals, orphanages, and other institutions of mercy resulted from obedience to the Bible.

Yesterday I drove to O'Hare Airport and took a jet to Washington without getting government permission. If my family so chose, we could move from Illinois to California without asking anyone. Freedom is a biblical concept.

Almost all good things of life that we take for granted bear the stamp of the Bible's influence—marriage, family, names, calendar, education, great books, magnificent works of art and music, freedom, justice, equal rights, the work ethic, the virtues of self-reliance and self-discipline, and on and on. The Bible has given us the noblest and finest in Western life and culture. Sir Francis Bacon said: "There never was found, in any age of the world, either religion or law that did so highly exalt the public good as the Bible."

So often I hear the silly statement that one religion is as good as another. An anthropologist once chided me in India: "Why do you want to introduce a new religion among tribal people. They're happy with the beliefs they have." I had to tell him that as an "insider," I knew they were not happy. I remember how it was before the majority of my people, the Hmars, accepted the Bible as their guide—the all night drinking parties to dull the frustrations of life, fighting in families, killing and stealing, and pitiful poverty. Having learned what it means to follow the Bible, the Hmars never want to return to the "happy" way.

My dear friend Cameron Townsend, founder of the Wycliffe Bible Translators, heard this naive objection hundreds of times. He would answer: "My friend, I fear you've never been closer to tribal people than the movies and television. If you could talk to those who have benefited from the

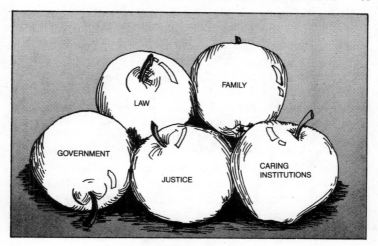

FRUITS OF THE BIBLE

Bible, they would tell you immediately that they were not happy, but miserable, in their old ways of life."

One of the most remarkable examples is the Aucas. Before missionaries gave them the Bible in their own language, this Amazonian tribe was moving toward extinction by constantly killing one another and by following a custom that required burying alive the children of a man killed in battle.

I remember so vividly when news came in January, 1956, that five missionaries were missing in the jungle in South America and feared dead from trying to reach these savage people. The story made the front pages of newspapers all over the world. Many remarked that the five missionaries had been foolish to risk their lives to get the Bible to the Aucas. But the *Portland Oregonian* editorialized after the bodies were found:

Unquestionably the effects of missionary work have not all been to the glory of God. But without the missionaries' zeal, Christianity quite probably today would have been merely a small sect of an older religion and would soon have ceased to exist. Few will argue that the world is not better for the spreading of the teachings of love and faith which are the basics of Christianity.

The forefathers of most of us were European savages or barbarians. Ulfilas brought Christianity to the Goths, St. Patrick to the Irish, St. Columba to the Scots, St. Augustine to the English. Boniface brought the Gospel to Germany, Ansgar to the Scandinavians and Vladimir to the Slavs. Would Europe and America be as enlightened today if these men had not felt that strange force which still sends missionaries forth to preach the Gospel to every creature?

After the burial of the martyrs, Elisabeth Elliot, the wife of one, and Rachel Saint, the sister of another, bravely walked into Auca territory and set up camp with this most feared group in Ecuador. The first five converts were the very men who had thrown the spears that killed their loved ones.

The book *Unstilled Voices* documents the Christianization of the Aucas, which followed translation of portions of the Bible into their language. The killing has stopped. The people are learning to read and write. They welcome visitors peacefully. Thanks to the Bible, love has replaced fear and hate, which were once their lot.

The Aucas are a small group, numbering only about 600 (they were down to about 200 when the missionaries came with the Bible). What about the influence of the Bible on the wider world? How has the Bible influenced the history of nations?

No group has been more influenced by the Bible than the Jews, principal characters of the biblical record. When they came into the Promised Land, after escaping Egyptian slavery, the Jews found themselves surrounded by pagan societies practicing child sacrifice, prostitution, and snake worship in religion.

God commanded Israel: "You shall not worship their gods, nor serve them, nor do according to their deeds; but you shall utterly overthrow them, and break their sacred pillars in pieces" (Ex. 23:24 NASB). Israel was to worship one God, Jehovah, and respect human life, parenthood, the marriage bond, and private property. The result was that Israel prospered and became the strongest nation in the region.

The Christian era brought the New Testament, which completed the Bible. The disciples of Jesus were indeed a light in the dark world of Greek and Roman society. The Epistle to Diognetus, probably the oldest of the Christian apologies (circa A.D. 125), aptly describes their biblical lifestyle.

> They marry as do all; they beget children; but they do not commit abortion. They have a common table but not a common bed. They are in the flesh, but they do not live after the flesh. They pass their days on earth, but they are citizens of heaven. They obey the prescribed laws, and . . . surpass the laws by their lives. They love all men, and are persecuted by all.

As Christianity spread across the Roman Empire, biblical influence on the sanctity of marriage and reverence for life increased, while polygamy, concubinage, and divorce decreased. Women rose in stature. Child abuse and infanticide declined.

The pagan Greek and Roman religions and the government of Rome permitted fathers to throw unwanted infants on garbage heaps. A common saying of the first century world was, "A man is a wolf to those he does not know."

Plato and Aristotle agreed that children should be abandoned when parents could not afford to rear them, or if they did not show physical and mental promise of service to the state. The Roman philosopher Seneca candidly admitted: "Monstrous offspring we destroy; children, too, if weak and unnaturally formed at birth, we drown. It is not in anger, but reason, thus to separate the weak from the sound."

Christians brought cast-off children into their homes. When the homes were full, the first orphanages were built and operated by Christian widows and deaconesses. But there were not enough Christians to care for all the unwanted children. Relief did not come until A.D. 315 when the Emperor Constantine, a newly professing Christian, decreed that parents must *not* kill newborn children. If they could not support them, government revenues were used.

Christians also took in thousands of the sick (even despised lepers) and homeless. Soon there were hospitals in every city with a sizable colony of Christians. Fabiola, a devout Christian and convert of Jerome's, established the first charity hospital of record outside Rome in A.D. 380. The great Jerome opened one at Bethlehem. The noted preacher-orator Chrysostom was responsible for several hospitals in Constantinople. It is no accident that the symbol of the medical profession is a staff entwined by coiling serpents, pointing back to the Old Testament healing of stricken Israelites in the Sinai wilderness.

Thalasius, a Christian monk, founded a home for blind beggars on the banks of the Euphrates River—another first. Christians opened the first asylums for the insane in Spain. Christians in Italy formed the first brotherhood of nurses, with Christians in other parts of Europe following suit. Modern nursing dates to these brotherhoods. Nursing by women was initiated by Florence Nightingale, who tended British wounded and dying during the nineteenth-century

Crimean War. The famed "lady with the lamp" was motivated by her Christian faith and the Bible.

Ministries of mercy were largely confined to monasteries during the Dark Ages when Catholic church policies effectively kept the Bible from the masses. The greatest reform and social services came after the Reformation, when the Bible was translated into many languages. Open Bibles opened hearts to suffering mankind.

John Howard, the sheriff of Bedfordshire, England, took a tour of jails and found prisoners branded, brutally beaten, and some with their ears cropped. Many were in jail solely because of unpaid debt and were not to be released until the last farthing was paid. Meanwhile, their families languished in abject poverty. "O Lord," prayed Howard, "visit the prisoners and captives and manifest thy strength in my weakness." John Howard launched a crusade to make prisons more humane.

Brave Elizabeth Fry put the Bible into practice for women prisoners. Appalled to find women and babies jammed into a dungeon in London's Newgate Prison like wild animals, she organized a band of ministering Quaker "angels" who taught the prisoners the Bible and the three R's, provided decent clothing, brought edible food, and pressured legislators to enact reforms.

British newspaper publisher Robert Raikes became concerned about the hordes of child waifs who scavenged and slept in the streets. In 1780 he paid a Mrs. Meredith, living in Sooty Alley in Gloucester, to teach children the Bible on Sunday in her kitchen. The children flocked there to study the Bible along with reading and writing.

Raikes is credited with founding the modern Sunday school movement, although the first Sunday school of record was initiated a few years earlier by Ludwig Hocker, a German Baptist, in Ephrata, Pennsylvania.

Inspired by the Bible, Anthony Ashley Cooper (also known as Lord Shaftesbury) set about to reform labor laws in Britain. Cooper, a member of Parliament, complained that children as young as seven were working from before dawn until late at night in factories and given only a cot and skimpy meals. He also called for legislation to shorten the "normal" 12–14 hour day for mothers, so they could spend more time with their families.

When some of his fellow legislators objected that government would be interfering with business, Cooper retorted that Parliament should be more concerned with "guardians of morality" (mothers) and "citizens of tomorrow" (children). Quoting Luke 2:52—"And Jesus increased in wisdom and stature, and in favor with God and man," Cooper presented the principle of "symmetrical growth." "Society," he added, "has a moral obligation to provide for the spiritual, physical, and social needs of the less fortunate."

In obedience to biblical commands, William Booth and his wife held open-air meetings and tried to help the poor in the squalid East End section of London. They organized their converts into a mission band that played, preached the gospel, and helped others in physical need. So came the Salvation Army.

The YMCA also began in England about this time. Christian workers began to hold prayer and Bible study fellowships for young Christian shopworkers in London. This movement later spread to America.

The biblical mandate to care was taken up by European missionaries at their far-flung posts. Where non-Christian religions permitted barbaric customs and ignored the plight of the sick and homeless, biblical faith brought social reforms, hospitals, leprosariums, and other compassionate outreaches.

England's William Carey, a missionary to India, crusaded against two cruel superstitions among the Hindus. Sick babies were commonly thought to be bewitched and left outside to die. Carey persuaded authorities that this was murder. Fearing arrest, many parents stopped the practice and, to their surprise, some of the babies got well. Carey also campaigned against *Sati*, which called for Hindu widows to be burned alive on the funeral pyre of their dead husbands. After many years, he finally was able to put a stop to this practice.

Biblical mercy continues to be extended to the ends of the earth by great Christian relief agencies. World Vision, founded by my beloved friend the late Bob Pierce and now under the leadership of Ted Engstrom, cares for hundreds of thousands of orphans and refugees and responds to disaster calls all over the globe. The World Relief Commission of the National Association of Evangelicals sponsors, in cooperation with missionaries, scores of relief projects around the world. In Bangladesh, the poorest nation on earth, for example, WRC has an agricultural collective that provides survival jobs for Muslim widows. These castoffs from Muslim society have nowhere else to turn, for the government and their religion provides no aid for widows.

Medical Assistance Programs, established by my good friend Ray Knighton, provides emergency medical aid abroad. Compassion, Incorporated, lives up to its name in providing for orphans and needy children in poverty-stricken lands. So does Christian Children's Fund. Food for the Hungry started by Larry Ward is saving multitudes from starvation. There is also Oxfam of England; Mother Theresa's loving care for the dying and Mark Buntain's hospital in Calcutta; Samaritan's Purse, founded by Dr. Bob Pierce and now headed by young Franklin Graham, son of the famous evangelist; and the TEAR Fund of Britain. And still I have left many other independent outreaches of biblical mercy unmentioned.

All the major Christian denominations minister to the

sick, homeless, and hungry. The Mennonites are loved around the world for their relief work and the young people they send from America. Southern Baptists and United Methodists have hospitals and programs for feeding the hungry. The Lutheran Relief Service, the Catholic Relief Service, and Church World Service (which channels funds from several denominations) serve the less fortunate in the name of the Nazarene.

When I was a student at the University of Allahabad in the Indian state of Uttar Pradesh, many of my fellow students enjoyed comparing the various world religions. I've since learned that Comparative Religion is a favorite course in Western colleges. Armchair academics like to argue philosophy and the differences in the holy writings of various religions along with the writings of agnostics and atheists.

When it comes to caring, only the Bible is left to stand on its feet. If you have traveled in Africa, Asia, and Latin America, going beyond the luxury hotels that tourists frequent, you know there is scant basis for the comparison of Christianity to other religions. As the minister of relief in Bangladesh told an inquiring journalist friend of mine shortly after the Bengali war of independence, in which so many hundreds of thousands were killed or left homeless: "Christians number only one-fourth of one percent of our population. But they are doing almost all of the relief work." In my homeland of India, Christians represent less than three percent of the population. Yet twenty-seven percent of all the hospital beds are provided by Christians and fifty-three percent of all the nurses come from the Christian community.

I would like to turn now to the influence of the Bible on the eradication of slavery. Some claim that the Bible actually helped keep slavery alive until modern times. Others say the Bible alone is responsible for doing away with slavery. Both views are too extreme. The Bible played the major role in eliminating slavery, but there were other influences, notably economic and political ones.

Until about two centuries ago, slavery was almost universally practiced. Some slaves were treated about the same as employees, except they could not leave their employer. Others were treated in a much crueler fashion.

Slavery was taken for granted in the Roman Empire. The Bible did not call for violent revolution to overthrow slavery. Even if it had, what chance would a few Christians have had against the Roman army? What the Bible did was light a time bomb under slavery by boldly declaring that all believers are equal in Christ (see Gal. 3:28). This teaching undermines not only slavery, but caste systems and mistreatment of women. At the same time Scripture also commands masters to be kind and protective of slaves and slaves to be more faithful to their masters. One of Paul's epistles asks a Christian brother named Philemon to receive back his runaway slave Onesimus "no longer as a slave, but more than a slave, a beloved brother" (v. 16 NASB).

Slaves rose to leadership in the early Christian community. By A.D. 140 an ex-slave was the spiritual leader of the Christians in Rome. The cynic Lucian observed, "The Legislator of the Christians has persuaded them that they are all brothers."

The drive to outlaw slavery throughout the world resulted primarily from the Protestant Reformation and the translation and circulation of Scripture in the world's great languages. In England the chief opponent of slavery was churchman William Wilberforce. In 1789 Wilberforce introduced a bill in Parliament to end the slave trade. When the bill finally became law in 1807, Wilberforce pushed for the outlawing of slavery itself.

"Read the Bible," Wilberforce repeatedly advised friend and foe. "Through all my perplexities and distresses I never read any other book."

French rationalists led the battle against slavery in French colonies. They attacked the evil practice on philosophical grounds, maintaining that all men have equal rights. Equal rights and human dignity are rooted in the biblical belief that man is created in the image of God.

The first antislavery society was established by Quaker Christians in England. The American counterpart was instituted in 1833 at Philadelphia and also led by Quakers.

From colonial times, slavery was opposed by almost all American church leaders. The Massachusetts legislature condemned the evil in 1641. The most influential evangelist of the first half of the nineteenth century, Charles Finney, campaigned for equal rights for both blacks and women.

Then in 1833 a Presbyterian minister, the Rev. James Smylie, set forth biblical "proof" texts to claim that slavery was divinely instituted. The idea seems weird today, but it wasn't the first time the Bible was twisted and misused for the wrong ends.

Under pressure from plantation owners and other Southerners who feared economic collapse if the slaves became free, many clergymen in the South bought Smylie's idea. Unfortunately, the Bible has a long history of being misinterpreted to support an economic or political theory.

Abolitionism captured the consciences of church leaders in the North. National denominations split. But public opinion in the North was not really aroused until the publication of *Uncle Tom's Cabin*, a book inspired by the Bible.

The author, Harriet Beecher Stowe, was the daughter of a minister, sister of a minister, married to a minister, and the mother of ministers. The crucial scene for her story about the misfortunes of the black slave Uncle Tom came to her while taking communion in church. "The Lord Himself wrote the book," she later said. "I was but an instrument in His hands."

Uncle Tom's Cabin sold over five million copies—an unbelievable number during the mid-nineteenth century. Many historians say this was the major catalyst in convincing millions of Americans, including some in the South, that slavery must be abolished.

Slavery is gone in the Western world, thanks largely to Bible-loving people. Racial discrimination continues strong in many areas, but in America the "back" of this evil was broken by the Civil Rights movement. Black clergymen, quoting the Bible, led this crusade. Again, opponents misused the Bible in trying to preserve discrimination, but the true teaching of Scripture prevailed.

Said Thomas Huxley, an agnostic: "The Bible has always been the Magna Carta of the poor and oppressed."

Let us now look at the Bible's influence on education. The fount of education is in the home. Research shows that the teaching and example of parents is actually more crucial for learning than the school a child attends. That's why I'm not surprised to learn that Wheaton College has a larger ratio of students going on to earn doctorates than any other college or university in Illinois. Almost all of the students at Wheaton and other good Christian schools come from Christian homes.

Mawii and I have tried to bring up our children by the Bible. We're proud of all three. Mary, our youngest, is a senior this year with outstanding grades at Wheaton Christian High School. John is among the better students in the senior class at Wheaton College. Paul is a doctoral student in math at the University of Illinois. Our children are not unique. Children in Bible-believing families tend to do better in school than the offspring of nonbelievers.

The Old Testament commanded Jewish fathers to teach their children "diligently" precepts on worship, family and social relations, skills in agriculture, and hygiene. ". . . talk of them when you sit in your house and when you walk by the way and when you lie down and when you rise up" (Deut. 6:7 NASB).

This helps explain why the Jews have given the world, in ratio to population, more great scientists than any other group. Let me illustrate: From 1901–39 only fourteen Americans became Nobel Prize winners in science while the Germans received thirty-five such awards. But from 1943–55 (no Nobels were given from 1940–42) the count reversed. Americans won twenty-nine Nobels and the Germans only five. This turnabout came because of the brain drain of Jews fleeing from Nazi Germany to the United States just before World War II.

It is not by chance that many of the world's greatest musicians, playwrights, novelists, newspaper publishers and columnists, and financiers have been Jews. Ann Landers and Abigail Van Buren are twin Jewish sisters. Adolph Ochs, founder of *The New York Times,* was Jewish. So was Joseph Pulitzer, founder of the *St. Louis Post-Dispatch,* the Columbia University School of Journalism, and the prizes for excellence in writing and photography that bear his name.

The influence of the Bible in education can partly be explained by the scriptural teaching that the home is the cradle for learning.

Now let us look beyond the home. What role has the Bible played in the development of classroom education?

The Jews established an early elementary school system after the Babylonian exile. Schools were developed as adjuncts to synagogues, with each community of 120 or more Jewish males expected to organize a ruling council and levy taxes for education. Attendance was compulsory for boys and optional for girls. The Law (first five books of the Bible) and the three R's were taught. This system continued after the Jews were driven from Palestine by the Romans late in the first century.

Christian education schools were opened in church buildings after A.D. 313, when Christianity became a legal religion in the Roman Empire. Schools to train monks, priests, and other religious workers continued in monasteries during the Dark Ages.

A big advance came during the reign of Charlemagne (742–814) when the powerful European monarch invited Alcuin, a devout Christian from York, England, to direct an educational program. Under Alcuin's guidance elementary schools were set up for children in local communities. So began the first movement toward general education. Some of these schools grew into theological seminaries; one seminary developed into the University of Paris.

The Reformation marked the beginning of compulsory, universal education. There was a burst of Bible translations, but what good was a Bible in your own language if you couldn't read it? The people cried for schools. In 1528, in the German province of Saxony, Luther helped begin the first system of compulsory, universal education. Similar educational systems, under the auspices of Reformation groups, sprang up across Europe, except in England where private Protestant schools flourished.

Reception of the Bible always whets a desire for education. Schools almost always follow.

Scholars of the Middle Ages and the Reformation period held the Bible in first importance. The greatest minds of the time were devout Bible students. Galileo ran afoul of church dogma with his correct views on astronomy, but he never ceased to believe in the Bible. Johannes Kepler developed a methodology of reporting scientific research that is still followed in scholarly circles today. Kepler, perhaps the greatest astronomer of all time, described his observations and calculations step by step, even noting where he went astray so that others could learn from his mistakes. Isaac Newton formulated the laws of motion without which space science could not exist today. These and other great scientists loved and believed in the Bible.

The launching of the modern missionary movement sped Reformation ideas on education to the far corners of the earth. The model was set by William Carey, the English founder of the movement. When Carey arrived in India he found no grammar textbook in any language. He prepared his own texts and translated the Bible into the four leading languages of my country and guided other translations into thirty-two more Asiatic languages. Carey put out the first newspaper ever printed in an Asian language and supervised the setting up of 126 mission schools and a college.

The present leaders of India, where only one person in about forty is even a nominal Christian, must admit that the nation's climb up the ladder of literacy and education is largely due to the Bible. Leaders of Africa, of whom many are Christian, concede that over 85 percent of all the schools on this vast continent were opened by Christian missionaries.

Education continues to be a fruit of missionary enterprise. The Laubach Literacy Crusade, founded by a Methodist missionary, has taught 300 million illiterates to read in over one hundred countries. Wycliffe Bible Translators has trained hundreds of bilingual teachers in South America and the islands of the Pacific. These teachers are certified by their governments and teach everything from the Bible and the three R's to carpentry, home economics, and health care.

Advances in agriculture go hand in hand with the Bible and education. There is a marvelous example of this on the Philippine island of Mindanao. Twenty-five years ago, a Filipino-Chinese Christian businessman, John Sy Cip, and an American missionary, Jared Barker, founded the Philippine Evangelical Enterprises. Today this Bible-based organization sponsors two colleges, two elementary schools, youth camps, health care programs (combining medicine and nutrition), and numerous agricultural projects. Thousands of people have been helped and a whole region transformed spiritually and economically.

Where would education be today without the Bible?

As to the Bible's influence on literature, I must start by stating that the Bible itself is the world's greatest literary masterpiece. The story of Joseph in Genesis is acclaimed as a model for short story writers. The Book of Job is recognized as the greatest epic poem ever penned. Said Thomas Carlyle of Job: "There is nothing written, I think, . . . of equal literary merit." Everyone has his favorite. John Adams, America's second president, called the Psalms "superior to all odes, hymns, and songs." Thomas Jefferson affirmed the Beatitudes to be the richest selection in all literature. Daniel Webster called the Sermon on the Mount the greatest legal digest in the world.

The Bible is the Book which has inspired countless other books. The great educator William Lyon Phelps declared: "The Bible has been a greater influence on the course of English literature than all other forces put together." Indeed, without the Bible the English language might not exist as we know it. When Wycliffe made the first English translation in the fourteenth century, Britons spoke almost 200 dialects. Often people in one village could not understand neighbors in the next. The spread of Wycliffe's translation, more than any other work, made English a common tongue. Likewise, Luther's Bible translation became the standard and unifier of modern German.

The greatest literary masters of Western literature perused the Bible for inspiration, ideas, and plots. One scholar listed 1,065 titles of English books of fiction, drama, and poetry not written for religious purposes. He found that 254 of the titles were quotations or adaptations from the words of Jesus in the Bible. DeFoe, Stevenson, Burns, Scott, Chaucer, Shakespeare, Browning, Milton, and Kipling are just a small sampling of the great writers whose works reveal the influence of the Bible. Robert Burns said: "Without the Bible my poetry would be woefully lacking."

Biblical themes continue to appear in the great works of the modern era. Four of many examples are Albert Camus's *The Fall,* Franz Kafka's *The Trial* (theme of judgment), William Faulkner's *The Sound and the Fury* (suffering), and Graham Greene's *The Heart of the Matter* (love).

Why has the Bible been such a force in Western literature? In the words of Henry Van Dyke: "The fountainhead of the power of the Bible in literature lies in its nearness to the very springs and sources of human life."

The influence of the Bible is even more evident in the greatest art, music, and architecture of the West.

From earliest times the Bible inspired great works of art. The frescoes of the Roman catacombs displayed the great biblical themes. When Christianity became a legal religion, Christian art blossomed in the churches and on the monuments of the empire. Through the nineteenth century, the greatest sculptures and paintings were based on characters or incidents in the Bible. The greatest artists—Raphael, Leonardo da Vinci, Michelangelo, Rembrandt, and others—are most appreciated for their biblical masterpieces.

With architecture the story is the same. The Notre Dame Cathedral in Paris, Westminster Abbey in London, St. Peter's Cathedral in Rome, and the National Cathedral in Washington are among the great structures that portray man's aspirations and worship of the God of the Bible.

What shall we say of the Bible's influence on music? The greatest oratorios, anthems, symphonies, hymns, and other classics have flowed from the Bible—Bach's *Jesu Joy of Man's Desiring*, Mendelssohn's *Elijah*, Handel's *Messiah*, Brahms's Requiem, Beethoven's *Mount of Olives*, and Haydn's *Creation*—to mention some of the best known. After hearing his magnificent work Haydn said, "Not I, but a power from above created that."

The Bible's influence on music continues, not only in classical works, but in hymns, spirituals, country gospel, and contemporary gospel and musicals. Think of ex-slave trader John Newton's much loved "Amazing Grace," country music singer-writer Marijohn Wilkins's "One Day at a Time," and Ron Huff's stirring praise arrangement "Alleluia," which echoes in thousands of churches.

What of the Bible's influence in government, law, and political freedom? Here also the Bible has proved to be a powerful force.

The Jews, obeying the Books of the Law, advanced from a disorganized mob of newly freed slaves to become, under David and Solomon, the most glorious nation on earth.

The Bible was first outlawed in the Roman Empire, then elevated, then taken as a basis for reforms by Emperor Constantine. Without these reforms, the empire might have fallen a century earlier than it did.

The Dark Ages descended when barbarians invaded and church leaders withdrew into their monasteries. Social needs went neglected, and the public good was disdained by church leaders who were more concerned about hanging on to earthly power than with giving the Bible to the masses.

Under Charlemagne, the Bible began emerging again as an influence in public life. Biblical principles of jurisprudence were written into that great monarch's Capitularies, sparking a move toward constitutional government.

A half-century later Alfred the Great, the Christian King of the West Saxons and a student of the Bible, saved his country from the barbaric Danes and introduced a legal code based on the Ten Commandments and other portions of Scripture.

Three centuries later, in A.D. 1215, the barons of Britian forced King John to sign the momentous Magna Carta, which placed the king under the law. A leading proponent for this revolutionary action was Henry DeBracton, a Christian judge, who developed the foundations of the legal system of present Western democracies. DeBracton used as his rationale the biblical doctrine of redemption, noting that God could have crushed Satan, but God chose to satisfy justice by sending Christ to die for man's sin. Justice, Judge DeBracton said, must take precedence over power—a revolutionary idea straight from the Bible.

Judge DeBracton's thesis, says Dr. Francis Schaeffer, a contemporary philosopher/theologian, became the basis for English Common Law. The Reformation then, according to Schaeffer, stripped away religious "encrustations" and positioned authority in Scripture alone "rather than church and Scripture, or state and Scripture."

Judge Blackstone, author of the famous law commentaries that until recent times were required reading in all Western law schools, affirms that "the Bible has always been regarded as part of the Common Law of England."

Under the Bible, England became the first power in the world. The three greatest periods of English history coincide with the times when the Bible was most highly recognized.

—During the reign of Alfred the Great England rose from barbarism, division, and ignorance into a united, civilized nation.

—During the reign of Queen Elizabeth I (the first monarch to promote circulation of the Bible; King James merely authorized a translation) England became a world power for the first time.

—During the reign of Queen Victoria, when the sun

Watkin Roberts, beloved missionary to the head-hunting Hmars, was the first to bring the gospel to Rochunga Pudaite's people.

Today 95 percent of the 125,000 Hmars are Christians who worship in tribal churches like this one.

Rochunga's aged father, Rev. Chawnga Pudaite, admires one of the first copies of the Hmar Bible, which his son (standing behind him) translated.

Every church can be a world mission center, and every member can take part by preparing Bibles for mailing, just as these people did at the Evangelical Free church of Willmar, Minnesota.

Bibles For The World is the only Christian organization allowed to mail large numbers of Russian Bibles into the Soviet Union. Here, Rochunga and an associate inspect a shipment of 20,000 Bibles ready for mailing from New Delhi, India, to Moscow.

Rochunga and his wife, Mawii, mail the millionth Bible to India.

Pastor Joe Mott of Austin, Minnesota, proudly shows off the pile of Bibles prepared for mailing by members of his congregation.

(L to R) Paul, Mawii, Mary, Rochunga, and John Pudaite

never set on an English possession, the empire reached its zenith. Asked by a foreign prince the secret of her country's greatness, Victoria replied, "The Bible, my lord."

France never rivaled England in greatness, although French rationalists, who rejected the Bible as divinely inspired, had noble ideas. The bloody French Revolution (1789–99) showed that rationalism could not provide the strong undergirding that England had received from the Bible. (England was spared such an upheaval, probably because of the biblical revival led by John Wesley.)

The agnostic Renan said in 1866: "If rationalism wishes to govern the world without regard to the religious needs of the soul, the experience of the French Revolution is there to teach us the consequences of such a blunder." Historians Will and Ariel Durant quote Renan in their *Lessons of History*,* adding: "There is no significant example in history . . . of a society successfully maintaining moral life without the aid of religion."

After World War I, the influence of the European colonialist powers began dissipating as the spirit of nationalism gathered steam in distant colonies. The Bible played an important role in the forming and shaping of many of these new nations.

Missionary preaching, Bible translation, and education in mission schools helped pave the way for the establishment of new nations. Johann Krapf, the great German Lutheran missionary to East Africa, refuted the idea that Africans could progress without European dominion by saying satirically:

> Do not think that because East Africans are 'profitable in nothing to God and the world' they ought to be brought under the dominion of some European power, in the hope

---

*Willard and Ariel Durant, *Lessons of History* (New York: Simon and Schuster, 1968), p. 51.

that they may bestir themselves more actively and eagerly for what is worldly and, in consequence, become eventually more awake to what is spiritual and eternal.*

The great majority of Africa's nationalist firebrands were trained in mission schools. Julius Nyerere, for example, attended mission schools and was the first of his country-men to graduate from a British university. When he led Tanzania to independence, the new nation was already one-fourth nominally Christian.

The Bible contributed greatly to the independence of Asian countries. The great Mahatma (meaning "Great Soul") Gandhi was leading his nonviolent crusade for free-dom when I was attending a mission high school in India. Before his death at the hands of an assassin, Gandhi de-clared that his ideas came from the life of Jesus and the writings of Thoreau. Gandhi said, "The Bible gives me great comfort and boundless joy."

Often I am asked, "What about Russia? If the Bible is so great, why did Communism take hold in such a religious nation?"

Religious, yes, but the Russian Czars who headed the state church did not promote the circulation and translation of the Bible. When Lenin came to power in 1917, the Russian masses were largely ignorant of the Bible, and evangelicals who proclaimed the Bible were being per-secuted by the state church.

Why is England so weak today, if the Bible is so power-ful? It is true that once-mighty England is now a second-rate power, plagued by rising crime, political unrest, labor riots, and breakdown of families. This is primarily because so many of her leaders have turned away from the Bible. A larger percentage of the people of the Soviet Union are said

---

*James and Marti Hefley, By Their Blood: Christian Martyrs of the 20th Century (Milford: Mich. Mott Media, 1979), p. 345.

to attend weekly worship and read the Bible than in England. The Bible is not the reason for England's decline; rather, misfortunes have come because most of the people do not take the authority of the Bible seriously.

The new *World Christian Encyclopedia* estimates that Westerners cease to be practicing Christians at the rate of 7,600 per day, while Africa is gaining 4,000 Christians per day through conversion from other religions, and three times that number through a high birth rate. In 1900, this authority notes, two-thirds of all Christians lived in Europe and Russia; by the year 2000, three-fifths will live in Africa, Asia, and Latin America. The influence of the Bible is shifting away from the Western world.

Without the Bible, Western society would not exist as we know it now. Sadly, secularizing trends have been carving out a widening channel in American culture since the turn of the century.

The winds of secularism—denial of absolute authority, departure from moral standards established in the Bible, and rapid diffusion of depraved and dissolute life-styles— are blowing at hurricane force in Western film, television, art, literature, and public education. The glory of God as revealed in the Bible, as writers Francis Schaeffer and Malcolm Muggeridge so painfully demonstrate, is departing from the West. Barring the return of Christ, nuclear holocaust, or totalitarian conquest, I expect that within the next century the West will eclipse into the paganism and barbarism of pre-Reformation times. But the Bible will not be left without a witness. God's banner will be lifted in other nations that choose to obey Him and follow the precepts of the eternal Word of God.

The Western nations—principally the United States, England, Canada, Australia, Germany, Norway, and Sweden— have been the leading force for world Christianization during the past two hundred years. But this flow of missionaries will be reversed, unless the tide of secularism is turned. I pray that Western society will learn the lessons of history and return to the Bible and the God of its fore-fathers. The greatest lesson to be learned is that the Bible, more than any other influence, is the Book that shapes history.

Chapter 5

The Book That Made America Great

THE GREATEST NATION in the world today is the United States of America. But when I was a boy in the jungle I did not even know there was an America. I thought the only white people in the world were the British. Then near the end of World War II, a young white soldier walked into our village and told us he was from America. I was puzzled. I thought perhaps he might be from some island off the coast of England.

Later, when I was attending Carey Baptist Church while a college student in Calcutta, I saw Americans almost every week. I noted they wore fine, white muslin short-sleeved shirts without ties. They would slap me on the shoulder and say, "Hi, how're you doing?" I thought America must be a very rich and friendly country. I wanted so much to go there.

One day I came back to my room and was handed a package from America. I opened it with great excitement. Inside was a beautiful leather-bound reference Bible with the inscription, "From a friend in America who loves the Lord and the people of India." Never had I seen such a fine copy of the Scriptures. I rubbed my palm across the cover. I examined the fine hand-sewn binding. I held the Book out before me just to admire it again. Everyone in America must be rich, I thought.

I read the Bible all the way through within about a month. I looked up everything I could find in reference books about America. If I could go to America, I thought, it would almost be like going to heaven.

I asked the pastor of Carey Baptist Church, Walter Corlett, "Do you have a place of service I can fill?"

"Well, Rochunga," he said, "you could be the secretary of our young people's group."

"I will be glad to serve," I told him.

"Good. The American evangelist Bob Pierce is coming here to speak next Saturday night. Bring all the youth you can find to hear him."

What a preacher! Bob Pierce made each of us feel we could do something for God that would make a difference. I wrote in my Bible, "Little is much when God is in it."

In the goodness of God, Dr. Bob Pierce and Mr. Watkin R. Roberts arranged for me to come to America. Soon after I got here, a train ticket came from Dr. Pierce. "You're going to be in America for a while, Rochunga. Use this to get acquainted with our country."

I set out by train from Chicago. Never had I dreamed I would take such a trip. In Philadelphia I visited Independence Hall. I stood in the very room where the Declaration of Independence and the Constitution were adopted. I saw the Liberty Bell and the verse from the Bible engraved on it: "Proclaim liberty throughout all the land unto all the inhabitants thereof" (Lev. 25:10). I felt I was standing on holy ground.

What wonders awaited in Washington! I strolled through the Library of Congress. I gazed up at the big letters across the Supreme Court that say EQUAL JUSTICE TO ALL. I walked the halls of the Capitol where the senators and representatives pass. I was even allowed to take a tour of the White House. No one stopped me. I could hardly believe this was possible.

I had read so much about the Great Emancipator that I wanted to see the Lincoln Memorial. I stood reverently

PRESIDENTS
AND
THE BIBLE

**"The Bible is the Book of all others
to read at all ages
and in all conditions
of human life."**

John Quincy Adams

**"All things desirable
to men are contained
in the Bible."**

A. Lincoln

**"It is impossible to
rightly govern the world
without God and the Bible."**

G. Washington

**The studious perusal
of the Sacred Volume
will make better citizens,
better fathers, and
better husbands."**

Thomas Jefferson

**"We are indebted
to the Book of books
for our national ideals
and institutions.
Their preservation rests in
adhering to its principles."**

Herbert Hoover

**"The Bible is
the moral code of
civilization."**

Harry Truman

**"The Bible is
the rock on which
our republic rests."**

Andrew Jackson

before the gigantic sculpture of the noble Lincoln, a man of the Bible. I read again his famous Gettysburg Address: ". . . resolve that these dead shall not have died in vain— that this nation, under God, shall have a new birth of freedom—and that government of the people, by the people, for the people, shall not perish from the earth."

In New York City I took the ferry to the Statue of Liberty. I saw such beautiful words inscribed in the pedestal:

> . . . Give me your tired, your poor,
> Your huddled masses yearning to breathe free,
> The wretched refuse of your teeming shore.
> Send these, the homeless, tempest-tossed to me,
> I lift my lamp beside the golden door!

Back in Manhattan, I took the elevator to the top of the Empire State Building and stared breathless at this great city. Then I traveled by train to California and whizzed past great steel mills, through bustling cities and sleepy towns, beside fields of golden grain, and across the majestic Rockies and into the sun-baked desert. By the time I got to Los Angeles, I had to stop and reflect on all the wonders I had seen. America was so big and wonderful.

Twenty-seven years have passed since my discovery of America. Never a day goes by that I do not thank God for this beloved country and its greatness.

What made America such a great nation? Is it her courageous pioneers and architects of freedom? Her vast natural resources? Her genius for technology, science, and agriculture that enables, for example, one farm worker to grow enough food for fifty-two people? Her diversity of immigrant-citizens? Her military might? Her colleges and universities that attract thousands of foreign students? Her democracy and freedom? Her opportunity for economic success? Her helping hands of goodwill to the less fortunate?

These, I suggest, are only manifestations of the real greatness of America—only branches on the mighty national tree that has given so much to the world. To find the source of a nation's strength and power you must dig into the foundations of its institutions. You must locate the tap root from which it grows.

The tap root of America is the Holy Bible. America, I believe, is the world's greatest nation because of the place and influence of the Bible in her growth from infancy to maturity.

All the historians and records I have consulted say that America was born and developed as a biblical, Christian nation. She may not appear so now. You would certainly not think so by watching television and looking at magazines on the newsstands. But America's *history* cannot be changed.

The documents of the colonies of early America shout the primacy of the Bible and Christianity. Maryland's charter declares that its settlers were driven by a "pious zeal for extending the Christian religion." Delaware's charter states as the purpose of its founding "The further propagation of the Holy Gospel." The Connecticut constitution bound its citizens "to preserve the liberty and purity of the Gospel of the Lord Jesus Christ."

In 1892 the Supreme Court made an exhaustive study of the relationship of biblical principles to the government, laws, and culture of the United States. The court noted that the state constitutions echoed the voice of the citizenry that biblical laws and ideas were part of the common law. The court went on to say:

> If we pass beyond these matters to a view of life as expressed by its laws, its business, its customs and its society, we find everywhere a clear recognition of the same truth. Among other matters note the following: The form of oath universally prevailing, concluding with an appeal to the Almighty; the custom of opening sessions of all deliberative bodies and

most conventions with prayers; the prefatory words of all wills, "In the name of God, amen"; the laws respecting the observance of the Sabbath; with the general cessation of all secular business, and the closing of courts, legislatures, and other similar public assemblies on that day; the churches and church organizations which abound in every city, town, and hamlet; the multitude of charitable organizations existing everywhere under Christian auspices; the gigantic missionary associations, with general support, and aiming to establish Christian missions in every quarter of the globe. These, and many other matters which might be noticed, add a volume of unofficial declarations to the mass of organic utterances that *this is a Christian nation* [my italics].

That opinion from the Supreme Court is taken verbatim from the case *Church of the Holy Trinity* v. *United States*, 143 U.S. 226.

In 1931 Justice George Sutherland reviewed the 1892 Supreme Court decision in reference to another case and asserted that Americans are a "Christian people." In 1952, Justice William O. Douglas, never known for traditional Christian beliefs, declared in *Zorach* v. *Clauson:* "We are a religious people and our institutions presuppose a Supreme Being." Yale's Dr. Sidney Ahlstrom, in his award winning *A Religious History of the American People* (Yale University Press, 1973) declares that America from the first European settlements had a "religiously oriented sense of mission."

One of the most important books ever printed is *The Bible in America* by P. Marion Simms, Ph.D. It was published in 1936 by the Wilson-Erickson Company of New York. Dr. Simms made an exhaustive study of the records of the various European nationalities that settled in America. He consulted with historians at the University of Chicago, Yale, Harvard, Princeton, and many other distinguished institutions. He paged through the files of the Bible societies, the leading Christian denominations, and the earliest missionary agencies. He looked at the Bible's influence on American law, government, and education. He concluded: *"No nation in all history was ever founded by a people so dominated by the Bible as America"* (italics added).

Consult the greatest scholars in America's universities and you will find them saying substantially the same. Even those who believe the Bible is only a great book, not divinely inspired, acknowledge the Bible's overarching influence. Dr. Robert Bellah, a sociologist at the University of California in Berkeley, chides secularists for seeking to "eradicate from public life" traces of religious belief. America's religious and biblical heritage cannot be denied, he says.

So great was the influence of the Bible during the American Revolution that a motion was made in the Continental Congress to make Hebrew the official language of the new nation. The colonists associated English with the British monarchy, while holding Hebrew in high repute as the queen of all languages, the key to understanding much of the Bible, and the foundation of a good education. They named many of their towns after biblical places—such as Antioch, Salem, and Bethlehem.

Hebrew was required study in many colleges and academies. Annual commencement addresses at Harvard were given in Hebrew until 1817.

The proposal by several members of Congress that Hebrew become the official language was voted down. But Hebrew, as well as Greek, the other major biblical language, continued to be required learning in universities for many years.

The Bible was studied in every school, from first grade through university. Yet Bibles could not legally be printed in America until after the Revolution. All Bibles came from the old countries, as Europeans came to America, bringing their translations in their native language.

Dr. Simms thinks Norse explorers brought the first Bible to America around A.D. 900. If true, they would have brought the Latin Vulgate translation. Greenland was discovered by 876, and bishops were appointed by the Pope in 1112 for Greenland and Vinland (thought to be New England). That was almost 400 years before Columbus.

Columbus probably brought a Spanish translation of the Bible on his first voyage. Catholic missionaries accompanied him on his second voyage and would certainly have had Spanish Gospels translated from the Latin Vulgate in 1490.

The first Protestants to arrive in America stepped ashore near present Beaufort, South Carolina, in 1562. A second group stepped ashore two years later. French and German Huguenots came fleeing religious persecution and hoping to set up a free Christian state in the New World. The French likely brought a translation of the Bible by Olivetian, a relative of John Calvin. The Germans probably had in their baggage the German translation by Luther. The Huguenot colonies did not survive. Many died from starvation and disease. The rest returned to Europe.

The chaplain who accompanied pirate-explorer Sir Francis Drake (son of a minister) probably brought the first English translation of the Bible to America. On the famous trip around the world (a first for an Englishman), the Drake expedition sailed into San Francisco Bay in 1579 to take on supplies. The chaplain probably used the Bishop's Bible, then the favorite in England, for worship services.

The first authentic record of Scripture in America places one or more Bibles in 1585 in the Virginia colony, named after the Virgin Queen, Elizabeth. Actually this was in present North Carolina, which was then included in Virginia. Captain John Smith asserts that the colony had a Bible. It was likely the Bishop's Bible. The historian Bancroft says that Thomas Hariot, a brilliant mathematician and devout Christian in the colony, "displayed and explained the Bible" in every Indian village he entered.

The Virginia colony also failed. The first permanent English settlement, as every American schoolchild knows, was established in 1607. Jamestown was named for King James I, who authorized the translation of the Bible that bears his name. Here the first Protestant church in America was organized.

The Jamestown congregation read from the Bishop's Bible or the Geneva Bible, translated under the direction of Pastor William Whittingham, a close friend of John Calvin. The Geneva version was the first to employ verse numbers and fill-in words (printed in italics) to make a literal translation easier to read. It was popularly known as the Breeches Bibles, because Genesis 3:7 was rendered, ". . . they sewed fig leaves together and made themselves breeches."

Dutch traders came ashore two years after Jamestown, probably carrying the Dutch translation of Luther's German Bible. Danes brought a translation in their language to New Denmark (northeastern Canada) in 1619. Swedish and Finnish colonists brought Bibles in their respective languages in 1638.

Fleeing persecution from their brother Puritans, the Pilgrim band landed at Plymouth Rock in 1620, over 700 years after the Norsemen set foot in the New World. The Pilgrims had the Geneva Bible, as did the more populous Puritans who staked settlements in their new Commonwealth of Massachusetts in 1629.

A galling trade restriction by Mother England forbade printing Bibles in the colonies in a European language. All Bibles had to be imported. But the Indians could not understand French or English. One day John Eliot, a missionary preacher, asked an old brave to pray. The Indian replied, "How can God understand me if he does not speak our tongue?" Eliot received special permission to prepare a translation in the language of the Massachusetts Indians.

A herculean task lay before John Eliot. First he had to analyze the exotic, tongue-tripping language, then prepare a grammar and dictionary. During the translation process he spent endless hours searching for Indian terms to describe concepts foreign to Indian ways of life. The Massachusetts Indians had no words for God, temple, father, heaven, and many other biblical terms. Eliot pressed on tirelessly. In 1663, after many trials and bureacratic delays, he was permitted to print his translation—the first distinctly American Bible.

A German Bible was printed illegally in the colonies in 1743. One or more English Bibles may have been printed illegally before the Revolution, but there is no clear record of an English version being published in America before 1782. Printed by Robert Aitken, this was the first and only Bible ever recommended for publication by an act of Congress.

Aitken's Bible was merely a copy of the King James. The first distinctly American Bible in English was translated by Charles Thomson and published in four volumes in 1808. A renowned scholar, Thomson had been the first secretary of the United States Congress and the one designated to notify George Washington of the Revolutionary commander's election to the presidency.

The freedom won by the American Revolution brought forth a tidal wave of Bible printing and distribution in America. By 1816 more than one hundred Bible societies were distributing Bibles. That year several of the societies merged to form the American Bible Society. John Jay, the first chief justice of the Supreme Court, was elected the first president.

In 1827 the ABS began providing Scriptures for foreign missionaries. Two years later the society launched a campaign to supply every family in the country with a Bible. Never in the history of the world had such a crusade been undertaken in one nation. The society printed Bibles in every major immigrant tongue. In 1846 the ABS began putting free Bibles into hotels, a mission later taken up by the Gideons.

The King James continued to be the most popular. Not until the 1870s did a team of British and American scholars attempt a major revision of the Bible in English. The new Anglo-American New Testament created so much excitement that the *Chicago Tribune*, the *Chicago Times*, and several other newspapers printed the entire new translation in a single edition.

Since the day the First European colonists unpacked a Bible on American soil, the Bible has increased in distribution and popularity. Many new Bible distribution agencies have emerged, including the New York Bible Society and the World Home Bible League. The Bible societies not only distribute copies and portions of Scripture throughout America and other nations, they also publish translations in minority languages for Wycliffe and other missionary translators.

Chicago real-estate broker William A. Chapman founded the great World Home Bible League near the beginning of World War II. As he lay seriously ill in a hospital, a Christian layman prayed that God would heal Chapman and call him into Christian service.

Chapman partially recovered and took a trip to Mississippi to regain his strength in a warmer climate. One night he and his wife stopped at a motel in the city of Biloxi. Picking up the Gideon Bible in their room, he said, "Betty, I wonder how many homes in America are without a Bible." Then he remembered the layman's prayer that he might be called into Christian service. That night Chapman vowed that if he lived he would put a Bible in every home.

Allied victory in World War II brought a new spurt in Bible publishing. Soldiers were returning from distant lands telling of miracles wrought by the Bible. One was a young naval officer named John F. Kennedy. The future president recalled that as his PT boat was sinking off a Pacific island, Christian natives came running to help him ashore, singing, "Jesus Loves Me."

Another soldier admitted rebuking a South Sea native who came proudly showing off his Bible. "We've outgrown that sort of thing," the American said.

The islander patted his stomach and grinned back. "Good thing for you that we haven't. If it wasn't for this Book, you'd be in here."

Hundreds of these American servicemen, who saw first-hand what the Bible had done among primitive people, became missionaries.

Twenty-five years after World War II, three liberal theologians made headlines by proclaiming that the God of the Bible is dead. Now hardly anyone can remember their names. Look at these sales figures for new translations during the last three decades: Revised Standard Version, 50 million copies; Living Bible, 26 million; Today's English Version, 12 million; New American Standard, 14 million. That doesn't include the King James Version, which continues to be the best seller of all Bibles in America.

There is no question that more Bibles have been printed and circulated in America than in any other country in the history of the world. But what difference has the Bible made in American history? How has the Bible molded the spirit and ideas of "America the beautiful?"

First, the Bible made America's founders believe that God had a great destiny for them. They were convinced that God was about to do something special in history. They were excited about being a part of God's great plan for America.

From this century we can see better than they the seeming hand of Providence at the time of the first settlements. The discoveries of Columbus and other explorers were stirring Europe. Multitudes were looking beyond the Old World with new hope.

Second, Europe was pulsating with revival fires fed by new Bible translations and printings.

Third, many Bible-believing Christians were suffering terrible religious persecution and looking for refuge.

Fourth, new political ideas were in the air. "Radical" scholars and politicians were saying that government should be for the people and by the consent of the people.

The time was right.

Thomas Carlyle dates the beginning of the "soul" of America to the landing of the Pilgrims in 1620. This little band of brave English Christians believed in democracy with responsibility. By their Mayflower Compact they were one for all and all for one.

> We are knit together in a body in a most strict and sacred bond and covenant of the Lord, of the violation whereof we make great conscience, and by virtue whereof we do hold ourselves strictly tied to all care of each other's good, and of the whole by every one, and so mutually.

This sounds a lot like the preamble to the Constitution which came over 160 years later.

Heart and soul, the Pilgrims believed they were part of a larger destiny. Governor Bradford wrote after they had put down stakes on the rocky shore:

> Thus out of small beginnings greater things have been produced by his hand that made all things of nothing, and gives being to things that are; and as one small candle may light a thousand, so the light here kindled hath shone unto many, yea in some sort to our whole nation; let the glorious name of Jehovah have all the praise.

The warm-hearted Pilgrims were more "low church" than the Puritans who began arriving nine years later. But the Puritans soon outnumbered the little band of Pilgrims and absorbed the smaller group. The Puritans saw themselves as the "new Israel" and sought to build an Old Testament society in New England.

Dissenters were not tolerated. Banished from Massachusetts in 1635, Roger Williams purchased land from Indians in present Rhode Island and set up a colony that guaranteed "soul liberty" to all. Williams founded the first Baptist church in America at Providence in 1639. His principle of church government is considered a model for democracy.

Thomas Hooker and three dissenting congregations fled in 1636 and established "an orderly and decent government according to God" in Connecticut. Their Fundamental Orders of Connecticut became the prototype for future democratic constitutions.

William Penn became the third member of the great triumvirate of democracy's forerunners. Penn's Frame of Government for Pennsylvania colony guaranteed every free man a vote and religious freedom.

William Penn said good men were the basis of good government. "Though good laws do well, good men do better, for good laws may [lack] good men, and be abolished or evaded by ill men; but good men never [lack] good laws nor suffer ill ones." Good men, Penn declared, would be obedient Christians. "Liberty without obedience," he stated, "is confusion," while "obedience without liberty is slavery." Penn was the first to call for a union of all the colonies and the first to propose a United States of America.

After the deaths of Hooker, Williams, and Penn, the colonies sunk into low morality. Only about one in twenty persons professed Christian faith. Drunkenness and sexual misconduct abounded. Crafty Europeans plied Indians with whiskey to dupe the red men out of their land. Slave ships disgorged thousands of tribal captives from Africa.

The light of the Bible flickered, then flamed high again as a stream of revivals called the Great Awakening brought cleansing and new moral purity from New England to Georgia. Bible preaching during the Great Awakening by Jonathan Edwards, George Whitefield, and other dynamic Americans provided a moral base for the coming Revolution.

From the Bible came also the revolutionary new idea of liberty. Daniel Webster said, "It is not to be doubted, that to the free and universal reading of the Bible in that age, men were much indebted for right views of civil liberty." Four centuries before the American Revolution John Wycliffe declared, "The Bible is for the government of the people by the people for the people." Centuries later Lincoln echoed that phrase in his Gettysburg Address.

Signing the Declaration of Independence in 1776 took more than ordinary courage. Thomas Jefferson, the principal author, and John Witherspoon, a Presbyterian minister, called on the "protection of Divine Providence" to secure the "certain unalienable rights" with which "all men are created equal" and "endowed by their Creator." The Declaration is a Bible-based document.

The Bible gave the outnumbered Americans courage to fight. A Congregationalist announced in a newspaper: "Brethren, we are in a good cause; if God be for us, we need not fear what man can do." It was against Quaker conscience to bear arms. But the Quakers supported the Revolution with relief work.

In the winter of 1777 the cause looked bleak. Many of General Washington's officers threatened mutiny. Starvation was predicted if the troops did not freeze to death first. Washington dropped to his knees in prayer, and from that time morale and strength picked up. The troops survived the terrible winter and emerged in the spring with stamina for victory.

The leaders of the new nation met in Philadelphia to write a Constitution. But they couldn't agree on many points, and it looked as if the body might dissolve in wrangling. At the darkest moment venerable Benjamin Franklin, eighty-three, stood and asked that "prayers imploring the assistance of heaven, and its blessings on our deliberations, be held in this assembly every morning before we proceed to business."★ Today, most official meetings in America are opened with prayer, from school board sessions to the United States Congress.

The American Constitution was framed by men—not all of whom were orthodox Christians—who believed in God and loved the Bible. The guarantees of freedom they wove into the Constitution go back to the Bible. Newspaper publisher Horace Greely declared: "The principles of the Bible are the groundwork of human freedom."

The Christian sabbath was recognized in the expression "Sundays excepted." If a bill passed by Congress was not returned signed or vetoed by the president within ten days, "Sundays excepted," it would become law.

The First Amendment did not separate government from God. It only says that "Congress shall make no law respecting an establishment of religion, or prohibiting the free exercise thereof." At the time several states, following patterns of Europe, still had "official" churches, while others did not. The architects of the Constitution wanted only to prohibit Congress from favoring one denomination over another.

America's founders could hardly have been more clear. Yet there are Americans who mistakenly believe that it is

---

★The spirit of the motion was well-received; but out of respect for diverse theological views and religious practices, the motion was not carried.

unconstitutional to have prayer before an official meeting. They would erase from coins and currency In God We Trust and dismiss all chaplains. As long as American courts pay attention to the original intent of the Constitution, I cannot see how such action can be condoned.

The ablest lawyers and legislators I know tell me the basic laws of the states and of the federal government are based upon the Ten Commandments and English common law.

No one is above the law. Senator Sam Ervin, former chairman of the Senate Watergate Committee, said, "Every man must stand equal before the law no matter how high or how low his place in society. And if any man goes out and violates the law, he must be punished like every other man."

The influence of the Bible is amply evident in American literature, music, and art, especially before 1920. I have never read an American poet, novelist, or essayist, writing prior to 1920, whose work was not influenced by the Bible. Take the gloomy Edgar Allen Poe, who is not one of my favorite writers. Dr. William Mentzel Forrest, a longtime professor of literature at the University of Virginia, analyzed Poe's works and found hundreds and hundreds of biblical quotations and allusions. Dr. Forrest said: "There is no mystery about [Poe's] familiarity with Scripture. He absorbed it from his environment; he met it in literature he critically examined; he was taught it in childhood and youth; he studied it in mature years."

I expect the same could be said about Whittier, Longfellow, Lowell, Emerson, and all other great American writers.

America's first books were religious books. Biblical themes permeated popular novels. Religious novels ranked among the top best sellers for generations. *Uncle Tom's Cabin, In His Steps,* and *Ben Hur,* all of the nineteenth century, are still considered classics.

The first was cited in a previous chapter. *In His Steps* is

Reverend Charles Sheldon's story of a small band of Christians who covenanted to follow as closely as possible in the steps of Christ. Their lives were forever changed.

Sheldon's novel began as a series of articles for a Christian magazine. He failed to copyright the story and thus the articles belonged to the public domain. The articles became a book, which, was published by over a score of companies, both in America and abroad. Few volunteered to pay the author royalties, but Sheldon was not bitter. The lack of a copyright, he believed, made the book more attractive to publishers. The millions of readers were reward enough for the Congregational minister.

Interestingly, a modern novel, *In His Steps Today*, follows the same story line, except the characters are twentieth-century people in a Chicago suburb. The author, Marti Hefley, says she read Sheldon's book at sixteen and waited twenty years for someone to write an up-to-date version. When no one came forward, she penned her story. The theme of biblical discipleship is timeless.

Lloyd Douglas, another Congregational minister, wrote several religious best sellers in the twentieth-century. *The Robe* sold in the millions and was made into a movie.

Ben Hur is better known as a film epic than as a novel. The movie is recent; the book was written by General Lew Wallace in the last century.

When he began his research of the life of Christ, Wallace "had no convictions about God or Christ. I neither believed nor disbelieved." The unbeliever Robert Ingersoll challenged Wallace to make up his mind. "Before I was through with my book," Wallace later wrote, "I had become a believer in God and Christ."

Early American art and music were attuned to the Bible. Modern popular songs often express hopelessness and encourage immorality. But much American music is Bible-based. I find it interesting that almost all the country music stars began their careers singing hymns and gospel songs in churches. Folk music often expresses the deepest beliefs of a people.

The Bible's influence on American education before World War II is of a magnitude that is hardly believable to those whose experiences are restricted to schools dominated by secular influences of the past thirty years.

For around 220 years, after the landing of the Pilgrims, almost all classroom education in America was Bible-centered and under the sponsorship of Christian denominations and associations. The first public school system in America was established in New York in 1633 by the Dutch Reformed Church and financed by tax revenues. Not until 1842 did the city of New York take over the Protestant Public School Society.

Quakers set up the public school system in Philadelphia. Puritans provided education for all children in New England. The preamble to the Puritan school of law of 1847 purposed to thwart the "old Deluder [Satan] that learning may not be buried in ye grave. . . ."

The alphabet, the Lord's Prayer, and a benediction were imprinted on America's first textbook, the famous *New England Primer.* Pupils learned the alphabet by catechetical verse, beginning, "In Adam's fall/we sinned all." They memorized Bible facts, verses, prayers, and the Apostle's Creed and learned Bible-based moral lessons from the *Primer.* Similar texts followed. One researcher surveyed schoolbooks up to 1776 and determined that 92 percent of the subject matter was permeated by biblical ideas.

For around one hundred years after the Revolution the texts continued much the same. The best known schoolbook of the early nineteenth century was Noah Webster's *Blue-backed Speller.* It began with this prayer:

No man may put off the law of God.
My joy is in His law all the day.
O may I not go in the way of sin.
Let me not go in the way of ill men.

The "American Schoolmaster" is most remembered for his dictionaries—which have been highly edited. Few Americans know that this choirmaster of a Congregational church encapsulated biblical ideas in definitions for his original dictionary. For example:

Hope   A well founded Scriptural *hope* is, in our religion, the source of ineffable happiness.
Love   The Christian *loves* his Bible. If our hearts are right, we *love* God above all things.

After Webster's works the *McGuffey Readers,* authored by a Presbyterian minister, were most popular. Total sales of the McGuffey series have reached 122 million copies and are now undergoing a revival of interest. The *Readers'* moral teachings are based on the Bible.

When public schools replaced private church schools, no one really became alarmed, according to historian Timothy L. Smith. "An evangelical consensus of faith and ethics had come to so dominate the national culture that a majority of Protestants were now willing to entrust the state with the task of educating children, confident that education would be 'religious' still."*

This expectation was too high. Secular thought gradually enveloped public education. Today the private Christian schools are again on the rise.

As for higher education, America's oldest colleges and universities were established by Bible-based denomina-

---

*"Protestant Schooling and American Nationality, 1800–1850," *The Journal of American History,* vol. 53, 1966–67, p. 687.

tions, primarily to train ministers. Look at this list: Harvard, 1636, by New England Puritans; William and Mary, 1693, Anglican; Yale, 1701, Congregationalist; Princeton, 1746, Presbyterian; Columbia, 1754, Anglican; Brown, 1765, Baptist; Rutgers, 1766, Dutch Reformed; Dartmouth, 1770, Congregationalist.

The last five schools were fruits of the Great Awakening. Dartmouth was founded to train missionaries to the Indians. Dartmouth's official seal proclaims *Vox Clamantis in Deserto* (the voice of one crying in the wilderness). And virtually all the elite women's colleges in the East (including Vassar, Wellesley, Radcliffe, Smith, and Mount Holyoke) were founded to train women for missions.

Many more colleges and universities were established after the Revolution by Bible-believing Christian denominations and organizations. Only a minority remain true to the intent of their founders. One of these is Wheaton College, founded in 1860. A leading abolitionist, Jonathan Blanchard, was its first president. Both Mawii and I received Bible-centered training at Wheaton. One of our sons is a graduate, and another will get his diploma from there this year. Another is Malone College, which graciously awarded me an honorary doctorate. There are others, of course, including a spate of new Bible-based colleges of more recent origin.

The Bible made America, in my judgment, into the most caring nation of the world. No matter what you've seen in the movies, America's founders did not first fall on their knees and then on the aborigines. The Pilgrim fathers invited the red men to their Thanksgiving feasts, nursed sick Indians, provided jobs, and taught the American natives the Bible. Some Americans did treat Indians badly, violating their women and cheating tribes of their land. It is unfortunate that we often hear only this side of the story.

For example, much has been made of the cruelty of

whites in driving the educated and Christianized Cherokees off their ancestral lands in Georgia and Tennessee and forcing them to march along the infamous Trail of Tears to Oklahoma. Hundreds collapsed in hunger and exhaustion and were left to die along the way. All this is true. But we don't hear so much about the dear Christian missionaries who fought the Cherokee removal and then walked the Trail of Tears with their brothers and sisters, offering consolation from the Bible.

Americans still give more money to charity than any other nation in the world. Many of this nation's charitable institutions have become secularized to the extent that some have almost lost their original identity. Organizations such as the United Way, the YMCA, and Goodwill have flowed from great outbursts of caring that followed national revivals. In response to the biblical mandate to care, Americans of the first half of the nineteenth century produced a league of societies to promote social welfare, fight slavery, help the poor, overcome drunkenness, combat injustice, and strengthen morality. They carried such names as the American Tract Society, the American Female Moral Reform Society, the Association for the Relief of Respectable Aged, the Fund for Pious Uses, the Philadelphia Society for the Encouragement of Faithful Domestics, and the Connecticut Society for the Reformation of Morals.

Nor do many Americans know that some of their greatest healing institutions were founded by Bible-believing Christians in obedience to Christ's command to heal the sick. Massachusetts General Hospital, Boston City Hospital, Philadelphia Hospital, and Bellevue Hospital of New York City are just four of many that were established by Christians.

There is not space to list all the caring institutions in America founded upon the Bible. Some are over a century old; some were only recently begun. One of the most noble recent efforts is Four State Christian Missions in Hagerstown, Maryland. A quarter century ago Jimmy and Ellen Resh opened a rescue mission for down-and-outers in an old house behind the city jail. They lived upstairs in a dingy apartment with five small children. From this beginning have come rescue missions in Hagerstown and seven nearby towns. The Hagerstown mission rehabilitates alcoholics, provides jobs for the unemployed, sponsors summer camps in the country for poor children, operates a chain of thrift stores, and serves as a relief agency for the whole area. Any burned-out family can come to the mission and get furniture and clothing for a new start. The mission's motto is: "If you haven't a friend in the world, you have one here."

Bible-inspired caring in America goes far beyond the many private institutions and organizations that serve the needy at home and on every continent. Even greater caring has been expressed in vast outpourings of giving and personal service.

On April 24, 1915, an estimated 600,000 Armenian Christians were brutally murdered by sword-wielding Muslims. Generous Americans gave over a hundred million dollars to the Near East Relief Fund for the survivors. The Bible prepared America for such generosity.

In 1921 Americans provided millions in relief to stave off mass starvation in Communist Russia. During World War II America gave billions of dollars worth of "lend-lease" supplies to Russia, China, and Great Britain. After the war America sent $13 billion in food, machinery, and other products to both former allies and *enemies* in Europe and Asia. America also took in hundreds of thousands of war refugees after World War II.

Following the ending of America's involvement in the Vietnam War, America received more thousands of refugees. At the same time Americans gave millions of dollars in food and medicine to stave off starvation among refugees in suffering Southeast Asia.

My country of India has received hundreds of millions of dollars of free aid from the United States. Whenever I hear one of my fellow citizens complaining about America, I stop to remind him of all that America has given away. The Bible, more than anything else, made America a caring nation.

You would expect me to say something about the churches in America and their great missionary programs. Sixty percent of Americans belong to a total of 331,065 churches. They give billions every year for Christian causes at home and abroad. Southern Baptists alone will have given almost one hundred million dollars to foreign missions in 1982.

I have not mentioned the material prosperity of America. A few small nations now have a higher per capita income than the United States. But more people are prospering in America than anywhere else. This prosperity, I believe, is the fruit of her Bible heritage.

Yes, America has problems. Many Americans have turned away from the Book of their forefathers. Yet in thousands of ways every day, both in America and around the world, the influence of the Bible upon this great country is still being felt. God bless America. May she return to her biblical heritage and her source of greatness.

Chapter 6

The Book
That Builds
the Church

A LONG TIME ago, before I even knew there was a land called America with towering city cathedrals and white clapboard churches at country crossroads, I was sitting in a small bamboo church in the little Indian village of Phulpui, listening to my father preach. For a number of days I had been thinking about becoming a Christian. "Ro," my father had said to me, "it says right here in God's Book that He will forgive you and accept you into His family if you will believe and take Jesus as your Savior."

Now Father was extending an evangelistic invitation. "If you truly believe and want to follow Jesus, you will not be ashamed to say so publicly," he declared.

I hesitated, looking around to see if anyone was watching, then I walked down the aisle between the rough benches. "My father, I want to give my name to Jesus. I believe, and I have asked Jesus to forgive me."

Father looked me straight in the eye. "Has He, my son?" he asked.

"Yes, my Father. If it is written in His Book that He will forgive those who ask Him, God would not lie."

"It is written in His Book." Father assured me.

Since that day when I set out to follow the God of the Bible, I have spoken and worshiped in some of the greatest churches in the world. I have seen thousands accept what the Bible says about forgiveness, salvation, and assurance. I have noticed that churches grow where God's Book is available and proclaimed, and that where the Bible is not central, churches do not grow.

The universal church, which includes all true believers, is a mighty oak that has grown from a little acorn. Sometimes when I get discouraged I take an imaginary trip back through nineteen-and-a-half centuries to that crowded upper room in Jerusalem where 120 believers were praying.

The last few weeks had been momentous beyond description. After a triumphal entry into Jerusalem, their Messiah, the Lord Jesus, had been arrested, tried, and crucified. Three days later He rose from the dead! For forty days more He was on earth, giving His disciples personal instructions. Then after telling them to wait in prayer for the coming of the Holy Spirit, He promised: ". . . you shall receive power when the Holy Spirit has come upon you; and you shall be My witnesses both in Jerusalem, and in all Judea and Samaria, and even to the remotest part of the earth" (Acts 1:8 NASB). The next thing they knew He was gone, ascended back to heaven.

There were only 120 believers in that upper room after Jesus had completed His earthly ministry and returned to the Father. How many are there now, believing, worshiping, serving Him on this great planet?

The latest and most accurate tabulation is 1,433,000,000. These are professing Christians. We have no way of knowing how many are true believers.

These figures are from the new *World Christian Encyclopedia,* which *Time* magazine calls a "bench mark in our understanding of the true religious state of this planet."* Dr. David B. Barrett, an evangelical Anglican missionary, spent fourteen years gathering information, traveling to 212 countries and consulting with 500 local experts in various nations in preparing his report for the encyclopedia.

From 120 to 1,433,000,000 is an increase of almost 12,000,000 percent!

But we can't congratulate ourselves—yet. This is still less than one-third of the world's population. The percentage of professing Christians to world population has been dropping since 1900 and will at present rates continue declining unless we find more fruitful methods and learn to proclaim God's Word more effectively to more people.

Here are the figures (in millions) from the *World Christian Encyclopedia:*

	1900	1980	2000
World Population	1,620	4,374	6,260
Christians	558	1,433	2,020
Percentage of Christians in world population	34.4	32.8	32.3

Three large belief groups have been increasing faster than Christianity and are expected to continue to outgrow the church.

Hindus moved from 12.5 percent (203 million) of world population in 1900 to 13.3 percent (583 million) in 1980. By the year 2000 it is expected that Hindus will comprise 13.7 percent (859 million) of world population.

Muslims have been growing even faster—from 12.4 percent (200 million) of the population in 1900 to 16.5 percent in 1980. At present growth rates Muslims will rise to 19.2 percent (1,201 million) by A.D. 2000.

---

*May 3, 1982, p. 66.

The fastest growing belief system in this century is classified "nonreligious and atheists." Starting with only two-tenths of one percent (3 million) of the world's inhabitants in 1900, unbelievers bounded to 20.8 percent (911 million) by 1980 and are expected to compose 21.3 percent (1,334,000) of mankind by the year 2000.

Christianity is losing ground fastest in the "Christian" West. Westerners are dropping out of the church at a rate of 7,600 per day, while Africa is reaping 4,000 Christians per day by conversion from other religions and gaining three times that many through the birth rate. As I have already noted, Dr. Barrett points out that in 1900 two-thirds of the world's Christians lived in Europe and Russia. By the dawn of the next century, three-fifths of the church will reside in Africa, Asia, and Latin America.

The biggest drop in the West is in Europe where Islam and atheism are making rapid gains. "Christian" Europe is becoming a vast mission field.

Dr. Barrett breaks down Christianity into four groupings. Since 1900 two categories—*Roman Catholic* and *"Other" Christian*—have increased their share of world population and are expected to continue going up. The Eastern Orthodox and Anglican communions have been steadily losing in percentage since 1900 and will continue this trend unless there is evangelism and renewal.

Mainline Protestant denominations (Episcopalians, United Methodists, United Presbyterians, American Lutherans, the United Church of Christ, the American Baptist Church, and a few others) show poor growth records. These denominations have been embroiled in theological conflicts and have been deemphasizing traditional missions in recent years. Conservative, evangelistic, mission-minded, and strongly Bible-centered groups are doing much better.

But in the Third World it is the *indigenous evangelical churches* that are growing the fastest. The Church of

Jotabeche in Chile has 60,000 members and eighteen pastors. Each week 15,000 members meet for prayer and street witnessing; 15,000 gather in homes for Bible study; 15,000 assemble in small prayer meetings; and 15,000 attend the church worship service (the building will only hold that many).

Could it be that Christianity is falling behind in population growth because we are not utilizing the basic Source Book that God has given the church?

The latest reports and research merely confirm what I've observed among my own Hmar people and wherever I've traveled throughout the world: Where the Bible is believed and freely circulated in the language of the people, the church goes forward. The Bible, more than anything else, builds the church. Where the seed of God's Word is faithfully and prayerfully sown and cultivated, the church grows. Many receive the good seed of the Word joyfully, allow it to take root, and bear much fruit (see Mark 4:1–20).

Every evangelical leader and authority on church growth agrees that this is true. When Simon Ibraiham, general secretary of the Evangelical Church of West Africa, received his first copy of the Bible in the Hausa language, he said, "It is important to remember that you cannot evangelize without the Scriptures . . . in the language of the people."

Morris Watkins, a Lutheran missionary leader, says, "We know of no permanent indigenous church that did not have the Scriptures in its own language and at least one church leader who was able to read those Scriptures or who had committed to memory a large amount of Scripture."

Dr. Sherwood Wirt, longtime editor of Billy Graham's *Decision* magazine, told me in an interview:

During my sixteen years as editor of *Decision* I wrote more editorials about the authority of the Bible than about any other subject. One reason was that I knew a lot of Christians were struggling with this question. Another was that for years I struggled with it; and not until I had been an ordained minister for eleven years did the Lord give me peace about my relationship to His Word. I ceased being a non-Bible person and joined the Bible people. I stopped being an authority on Scripture because I learned that Scripture was in fact an authority on me.

I think of the Bible not as a relic, or an artifact, or a record of a historical movement. I think of the Bible as a rapier of steel, to be seized and used to pierce men's consciences and to ward off the enemy. God never intended His Word to be bound in morocco and placed on a shelf. He did not send it to the world for the convenience of clergymen or the edification of scholars. He did not send it to keep kings in power. He wrote the Bible for you and me, and He sees to it that the message is trustworthy.

Dr. Billy Graham's power is in the Bible. How many times have you heard him declare, "The Bible says . . ."? All the great evangelists and pastors I have ever read or heard were men of the Bible. The Bible has been the Book that built the church from the first century until now.

Return with me to Jerusalem in the first century. As the 120 followers of Christ waited in prayer, a multitude of devout Jews speaking eighteen languages arrived for the Feast of Pentecost.

Suddenly there was a roar like a violent, rushing wind that filled the whole house. Everybody was startled. Dancing tongues of fire lighted on the disciples as they proclaimed the Good News that Jesus died and rose from the dead.

The foreign visitors were amazed: "And how is it that we each hear them in our own language to which we were born? . . . What does this mean?" Others, mocking, said, "They are full of sweet wine" (Acts 2:8,12,13 NASB).

Peter, the spokesman for the 120, stood to explain:

"These men are not drunk, as you suppose, for it is only the third hour [nine A.M.] of the day; but this is what was spoken of through the prophet Joel . . ." (Acts 2:15,16 NASB). Peter proclaimed the Bible (see vv. 17–36), setting the precedent for the growth of the church from the sowing of the seed.

That very day 3,000 souls were added to the church (see v. 41). The next verse reads, "And they were continually devoting themselves to the apostles' teaching and to fellowship, to the breaking of bread and to prayer." They first gave attention to the apostles' teaching—the oral Word of God, for the New Testament was not yet written down. What was the result? "The Lord was adding to their number day by day those who were being saved" (v. 47 NASB).

One afternoon, a few days later, Peter and John were entering the temple for prayer when a lame beggar asked them for money. (This has happened to me many times in Asia. I never know quite what to say.) "Look at us!" Peter commanded (Acts 3:4 NASB). The beggar lifted his eyes expecting a coin. "I do not possess silver and gold, but what I do have I give to you: In the name of Jesus Christ the Nazarene—walk!" (v. 6 NASB). Peter seized the beggar by the right hand and pulled him up. The beggar felt strength returning to his withered limbs and began "walking and leaping and praising God" (v. 9 NASB).

People came running from everywhere, giving Peter another opportunity to proclaim the Bible: "But the things which God announced beforehand by the mouth of all the prophets, that His Christ should suffer, He has thus fulfilled" (v. 18 NASB).

Peter referred them to Deuteronomy 18:15,18 where Moses predicted: "The LORD God shall raise up for you a prophet like me from your brethren; to Him you shall give heed in everything He says to you" (Acts 3:22 NASB).

This time 5,000 men, not counting women and children,

were converted (see Acts 4:4). What marvelous church growth! Eight thousand new male believers within days, plus the additions mentioned in 2:47.

So it goes throughout the thrilling saga of the early church as recorded in Acts. When persecution came, forcing the new believers to scatter, what happened? They went "every where preaching the Word" (8:4). The Bible is the Book that builds the church.

As goes the Bible, so grows the church. During the early centuries the church grew rapidly in the Middle East. But the Bible soon took a back seat, and a powerful Islamic tide almost wiped out Christianity in that region. Many great church sanctuaries were converted to mosques. Churches that survived were forbidden to evangelize. This situation persists in many of these countries today.

How did it happen? Historians cite a number of reasons: When persecution stopped, the church became more comfortable, centralized, bureaucratic, political, and indifferent to the missionary mandate. Doctrinal quarrels and power struggles among church leaders chilled the spirit of love. Pagan "mystery" cults moved in to lead many Christians astray. The Roman Empire weakened and split in half, bringing political uncertainty. But none of those reasons is the main one for the church's being almost wiped out in the cradle of its birth. It was *the failure of church leadership to translate and distribute Scripture into the indigenous languages.*

This tragedy continued until the Reformation. In "Christian" Europe, where the Muslims were turned back, Bible reading had been confined to monasteries and bishops' palaces. The Reformation broke down the doors and freed the Word of God for translation, printing, and distribution.

Still it was almost 200 years before the church regained its burden for world missions. William Carey, the shoe cobbler turned preacher, addressed a Baptist ministers' meeting in 1792 on the topic: "Whether or Not the Great Commission

Is Binding Upon Us Today." The moderator rebuked him: "Sit down, young man. When God pleases to convert the heathen, He will do it without your aid or mine."

Ignoring such objections, Carey took the Bible to India. He engaged himself in learning the major languages of India in order to translate the Bible into these tongues.

Carey founded the modern missionary movement. Around 65,000 trained, career Protestant missionaries are stationed outside their home countries today. Fifty-six percent of these, according to P. J. Johnstone's handbook *Operation World,* are from the United States, which provides 90 percent of all funds for world missions. Some 10,000 to 15,000 missionaries are supported from outside North America and Britain.

To these we must add Campus Crusade's 14,500 staff members, making a total of almost 80,000 missionaries. We can assume that one-fourth of the 80,000 will be home on furlough at any given time, some for as long as a year. This leaves 60,000 active on fields of service. To these let us add an estimated 15,000 short-term workers who go to assist the career missionaries. This brings the number back up to 75,000 missionaries, assigned to 4,374,000,000 people—an average of one for every 58,320 persons in the world.

However, at least half, if not more, of these 75,000 are not engaged in seed sowing and harvest. They are doing very good work as teachers, doctors, nurses, and agriculturists, but they are not giving full-time attention to personal evangelism, preaching, broadcasting, and Bible and literature distribution. This brings us to one missionary evangelist for every 116,640 persons.

What results are our missionaries getting? How many people are they winning to Christ and bringing into national churches? This is difficult to determine since some missionary agencies report "decisions for Christ," while others record only convert baptisms.

The aggressive Foreign Mission Board of the Southern Baptist Convention publishes well-kept records of baptisms by Baptist churches to which their missionaries minister on the foreign field. Most of the baptisms are by national pastors, however, making it difficult to determine how much of a part the missionaries played in direct evangelism.

With 3,059 missionaries, the Southern Baptists reported for the year 1980 a total of 110,032 baptisms in ninety-four countries. Baptisms by churches that send missionaries from the United States and Canada are not included. Southern Baptists led all non-Catholic denominations by baptizing 429,742 converts in the United States.

The Southern Baptists' report for 1980 shows 13,606,808 registered members. They have one foreign missionary for every 4,452 church members. The total membership gave $79,617,895 for foreign missions in 1980, an average of a little less than $6 per member. To turn one more figure, it cost the Southern Baptists in 1980 an average of $724 per baptized convert to maintain their missionary thrust on the foreign field, with contributions coming from about 120 home churches.

Some smaller groups, notably the Christian and Missionary Alliance, do much better on the average. At the same time many, if not most, Protestant denominations have fewer missionaries, recording fewer convert baptisms in ratio to current membership, than do the Southern Baptists.

Figures sound cold, but they are necessary to tell us what is happening. I thank God for every faithful missionary and for every person won to Christian faith in every country. Mawii and I encourage and support the foreign missionary program of our local church. We want to send more missionaries.

Another important point I would like to set forth is the outreach of our missionary programs. Where are our missionaries going? What fields receive the most attention? What populations are given priority?

Some missionary groups are specialists by calling. The Laubach Literacy Crusade concentrates on illiterates. Missionary Aviation Fellowship provides flying service for missionaries and national churches. Wycliffe Bible Translators' avowed goal is to provide at least the New Testament for every unwritten language.

A total of 5,103 languages are known to be spoken in the world. About 3,000 of these are unwritten. Wycliffe now has 4,500 workers laboring on 725 languages. Wycliffe workers have translated one complete Bible, 157 New Testaments, and 440 Scripture portions into remote languages.

Wycliffe folks are true pioneers. They serve the whole church, sometimes at unbelievable sacrifice. Many Wycliffe members work for five to ten years without seeing one person come to Christ. You can imagine how long it takes to learn a strange language, prepare a grammar and a dictionary, then translate Scripture that the tribal people can understand.

But when the harvest comes, sometimes it is very great.

Some forty years ago a young Wycliffe member named Bill Bentley went to the Mexican state of Chiapas, bordering Guatemala, where he intended to translate the Bible for the Tzeltal (pronounced ZEL-tal) Indians. On a trip back into the jungle, he met a Tzeltal chief who spoke a little Spanish.

"Do you know about a Book from God?" the old chief asked.

"I do," Bentley smiled, "and I have come to learn your language and give you God's Book."

The chief gave Bentley permission to enter his tribe. But the young translator died of a heart attack at twenty-seven, six days before his wedding date. His fiancée, Marianna

Slocum, and another young woman came to replace him. After many trials and difficulties, they completed the Tzeltal New Testament twenty-four years later, and it was published by the American Bible Society. Near the same time, other Wycliffe workers completed the New Testament for the neighboring Chol Indians. It too was published by the ABS.

After the Tzeltals and Chols found that "God speaks our language," over 25,000 of these Indians became Christians. Hundreds of farmers found the courage to apply for homestead tracts on which to grow coffee. Before the Bible came they toiled for eight cents a day for big land owners who controlled the land and threatened punishment for farmers who dared apply for land. Thanks to the Bible, hundreds of churches sprang up, and the whole area was transformed spiritually, morally, economically, and educationally.

I could cite many more examples of the results of Bible translation and publication among remote tribes. Recently news came from Ecuador of a Bible-inspired "revolution" among Quechua Indians in the Andes Mountains. Gospel Missionary Union translators worked for almost fifty years there before the blessed harvest came. Where there had been only a dozen or so believers, now there are over 25,000, plus two Christian radio stations operated by nationals and a network of schools—Bible institutes that train preachers and offer agricultural courses for farmers. Another side effect of the Bible among the Quechuas is moral reform. Sobriety has replaced mass drunkenness in many villages. Illegitimate births have dropped sharply.

Because I was first a Bible translator before becoming a Bible distributor, I feel a close kinship to the missionary linguists who make God's Word available for the first time to primitive tribes and other minority language groups. Still I must admit that the bibleless tribes represent only about 2 percent of the world's population. When there is a Bible in every language—may God speed that day—the world will still not be evangelized.

One of the missionary researchers and planners I greatly admire is Dr. Ralph Winter, general director of the Center for World Mission. Dr. Winter and missionary specialists at Fuller Theological Seminary and World Vision have identified 16,750 "Hidden Peoples," who have no churches and have been almost entirely overlooked by mission agencies and national Christian leaders. The Bible is already available in most of the languages that these groups speak; it has just not been taken to them. These are not small groups of a few hundred people. Some number in the millions.

Dr. Winter estimates that 95 percent of all career Protestant missionaries are working among three categories of people: existing churches, newly founded churches, and in cultures where the gospel has already penetrated. Only one of every 171 full-time Christian workers is trying to reach the Hidden Peoples.

Not long ago world evangelical leaders met in Thailand and called for 200,000 missionaries by the year 2000. Doubters say that this goal is not reachable without a great spiritual awakening in North America.

Groups such as the Southern Baptists, who are aiming to have 5,000 missionaries on the field by the year 2000, have worthy goals. But the record of the past few years among evangelical groups suggests that the doubters are the most realistic. Allen Finley and Lorry Lutz, in *Mission—A World Family Affair,* note that in 1978 the Interdenominational Foreign Missions Association (IFMA), with forty-nine member agencies, reported a total career missionary force of 10,662 missionaries (including missionaries serving in home offices). By 1980 the IFMA missionary force had grown to 10,679, a net gain of only 17 persons in two years. The Evangelical Foreign Missions Association (EFMA), with eighty-one member organizations and 7,632 career missionaries, *declined* in personnel by two-tenths of one percent over the same period.

What of the great missionary-supporting churches? Dr. Harold Ockenga served the famous Park Street Congregational Church of Boston for forty years before retirement. While he was pastor, that church supported 142 missionaries at a cost of $250,000 a year. Park Street Church now, according to Dr. Ockenga, supports only seventy-two missionaries for $510,000 at $7000 per person. Of course, other churches and individuals join in the support of these missionaries. Presently it costs an average of $30,000 a year to keep a missionary family on the field. With only mild inflation, that figure will jump to over $100,000 by A.D. 2000.

I could go on citing other figures and examples to support the thesis that vast numbers of people are not receiving the Bible, which is the most essential ingredient for building strong churches.

Why, it would take 4,000 missionaries 1,000 years to speak just once to everyone in India about Christ, even if the population stopped growing at the present rate of over a million persons each month! We simply cannot reach the world by depending on missionaries alone.

This thesis is not unique with me. Missionary leaders have been talking about the unreached for more than a generation. Dr. Winter especially keeps prodding the church to accept the challenge of the worldwide missionary task.

What about electronic media? Isn't everybody now within the "sound" of the gospel by television, radio, or player cassette? If this isn't so, won't this be true in just a few years?

The electronic media has brought us almost to the age of Buck Rogers. Theoretically it is possible to send Christian programs by satellite into every home on earth. The technology is here. Yet this is not likely to be a reality for many years, if ever.

The first problem is that every home must have a TV set. In most underdeveloped nations a satellite dish will be required to bring down the signal. There is an average of two radios in every American home and a television set for at least every two Americans. But the figures below, taken from the December 1981 *Geo* magazine, show that broadcast sets are not so abundant in most countries.

Country	TVs	Radios
	(per 1,000 people)	
Argentina	117	384
Australia	357	1,037
Austria	262★	275
Bangladesh	0	6
Congo	2 .4	61
Cuba	83	197
Denmark	471	825
E. Germany	325	895
Egypt	26	136
Ethiopia	1	7
Finland	400★	398
France	278★	330★
Greece	117	296
Honduras	17★	57★
India	1	33
Ireland	215	300★
Israel	137★	208
Italy	225	236
Japan	242	571
Kenya	4 .2	37
Kuwait	478	487
Lebanon	147	540★

Country	TVs	Radios
	(per 1,000 people)	
Mexico	84	276#
Netherlands	325	614
Nigeria	7	79
Pakistan	8	66
Paraguay	20	67
Philippines	19	43
Poland	207	241
Puerto Rico	162	549★
Qatar	2,041	316#
Saudi Arabia	32	29
S. Korea	96	400
Soviet Union	143	390#
Sweden	370	1,005
Thailand	17	129
Turkey	54	101
Uganda	7	20
U.K.	390	716
U.S.A.	623	2,048
W. Germany	300★	332★

1970 figures   ★1976 figures

The number of radios is much less in many areas of some countries. The tabulation above shows India has thirty-three radios per thousand population. Once I was in New Delhi, and the head of the government broadcast service asked me to give a fifteen-minute goodwill broadcast for the Mizo tribal people of northeast India. I asked him, "Out of 100,000 how many do you think will have radios?" He said, "Oh, maybe about 200." Then I remembered hearing a Christian broadcaster say that he was "blanketing" that whole area with the gospel.

The second reason the world cannot be reached by Christian broadcast media within the next few years is that gospel programs are available in so few languages. I would guess that 95 percent of all religious broadcasting is in English. I thank God for the outreach of missionary broadcasting and cassette ministries. Trans-World Radio, the Far East Broadcast Company, the Christian Broadcasting Network, PTL, Trinity Television, and other ministries are doing great work. I commend the effort of all Christian broadcasters. But the world is not going to be won by electronic media alone. And I have not mentioned cultural problems in communication and the impermanence of a heard or seen message.

What about missionary literature? Well, I know of no one doing more than World Literature Crusade. WLC is entering its thirty-fifth year and is distributing good Christian reading material in fifty-six countries, with plans to advance into eighteen other nations. The last report I saw indicated that WLC, with a staff of 1,566, has distributed 1,250,274,050 pieces of literature and received 10,566,896 cards recording a spiritual decision of some sort. Other groups are also getting the biblical message out with literature and are achieving wonderful results.

Thank God for missionary literature. We're just waking up to the fact that Communists are providing most of the reading material for many persons whom Christians have taught to read. In India 70 percent of all literature reportedly comes from Communists.

I would, however, make this comment. A tract or booklet represents some particular interpretation and application of Scripture. There is even subjectivity in the verses chosen for a Scripture tract. The finest literature cannot replace the pure Word of God.

The Bible is the best missionary tool for evangelizing the world and for building the church. "The Word of God is living and active and sharper than any two-edged sword, and piercing as far as the division of soul and spirit, of both joints and marrow, and able to judge the thoughts and intentions of the heart" (Heb. 4:12 NASB). God promises, "So shall My Word be which goes forth from My mouth; / It shall not return to Me empty, / Without accomplishing what I desire, / And without succeeding in the matter for which I sent it" (Is. 55:11 NASB).

The Bible is really more than a tool. It is the best of all missionaries. One day I was reflecting on this great truth and felt a sudden surge of inspiration. I wrote:

I have seen hundreds of missionaries both at home and abroad, but I want to tell you of the missionary I love most. He has deeply influenced my heart and greatly enriched my life. He is the missionary after my heart, and God's heart too. Given a chance, he would conquer the world within our generation.

Surprisingly, this missionary idol of mine is the frailest of all missionaries I have met. He looks thin, ill clad, despised. He can hardly stand upright and spends most of his days leaning upon others. He cannot walk a block unless transportation is provided for him. He sits speechless most of the time, though he loves to talk to someone. He loves to be handled like a little child, but he is so frail that a child can mistreat him or a drunken man can trample him under his feet. I have seen this amazing missionary at work. Fifty years ago he was sent to India to evangelize a sin-degraded, headhunting mountain people. When he arrived in the village, the chief examined his credentials and issued him a permit to stay. Before long, everyone was impressed with his message, and night after night people came to see him. He was so humble that everyone loved him. His long-suffering and gentleness especially impressed the people. He was calm even when the children handled him roughly.

Before long five men, including the chief, announced their willingness to accept his message. Since that day, the missionary has multiplied his witness a thousand times. He has learned many new languages while traveling much of the time. He has had the joy of seeing over two hundred indigenous churches established and has had a part in winning thousands of souls to Christ. I have known him for the past twenty-five years, and the more I work with him, the more I love and appreciate Mr. Written Word.

For many years I wondered how many copies of Mr. Written Word had been distributed.

The Old Testament was available in both Hebrew and Greek before the coming of Christ. The twenty-seven New Testament books were all written by A.D. 90. For the next 1,360 years, all Bibles had to be copied by hand. Almost all of the complete Bibles were in the possession of scholars, monks, and high church officials. Few Christians ever so much as saw a complete Bible.

Almost certainly more Bibles came off the presses during the fifty years after Gutenberg than were hand-copied and distributed during the past fourteen centuries. Since the advent of the printing press, millions upon millions of Bibles and Testaments have been sold or given away. Thousands of church groups and organizations have printed Bibles. Many kept no records. Many have long since ceased to exist. The exact number of Bibles and Testaments printed can only be known by God.

The American Bible Society is the world's single biggest publisher and distributor of Bibles. Clifford P. Macdonald, editor of the *American Bible Society Record*, reports that as of December 31, 1981, the ABS had distributed during the past 165 years exactly 3,396,127,592 Bibles, Testaments, portions, and selections of Scriptures. A large majority of these are portions and selections of Scriptures.

Macdonald further notes that as of the end of 1981 the Bible had been translated in whole or in part into 1,739 languages. The full Bible is in 277 languages, the New

Testament in 518, and at least one complete book of the Bible is available in 944 languages.

In just fifteen years Living Bibles International, the missionary ministry founded by Dr. Ken Taylor, has published over 16 million New Testaments in 35 languages, 300,000 complete Bibles in 4 languages, and several million portions in 71 other languages. LBI is presently working in 107 languages and has plans to publish in 78 more during the next ten years. As Dr. Taylor did with his *Living Bible* in English, LBI endeavors to communicate the meaning of the original biblical text in the idiom of the average person.

United Bible Societies represents Bible distribution agencies in many nations. The UBS reports the following worldwide distribution by member societies during 1980:

Bibles	9,653,508
Testaments	13,915,505
Portions	28,044,595
New Reader Portions	7,325,876
New Reader Selections	32,990,638
Selections	348,124,661
Total for world	440,054,783

Note that only about 5 percent of the above are complete Bibles and Testaments. These figures represent *most* of the major Bible societies of the world.

The UBS presents a breakdown distribution by countries. Note the figures for Bangladesh, which has 92 million people:

Bibles	6,393
Testaments	8,397
Portions	58,702
New Reader Portions	362,067
New Reader Selections	766,411
Total for Bangladesh	1,201,970

Slightly fewer than 15,000 Bibles and Testaments were distributed by the Bibles societies among 92 million people.

Assuming zero population growth, all the people now alive in Bangladesh would have to live six thousand years before they would receive a Bible or Testament at this rate of distribution.

After adding up all the figures I can find on Bible distribution, I cannot claim an accurate tabulation. I can only make a rough estimate that 2,100,000,000 Bibles and New Testaments have been printed since the Gutenberg Bible was published in A.D. 1451.

I praise the efforts of the Bible societies. What they do is of immeasurable worth to the kingdom and church of God. But the gap remains in Bible distribution, and it becomes wider every year.

Here is another startling fact that should jar every Christian: *Eighty-five percent of all Bibles printed today are in English for the nine percent of the world who read English. Eighty percent of the world's people have never owned a Bible while Americans have an average of four in every household.*

The biggest block is distribution, not translation. The entire Bible has been translated into the languages of 90 percent of humanity, the New Testament for another 5 percent, and at least one Bible book for 3 percent. This leaves only 2 percent with no Scripture whatsoever.

William Carey's translation in Hindi has been available in India for 160 years. Yet only one-and-a-half million copies have ever been printed and distributed. Today there are over 375 million Hindi speakers in my country.

Bibles are sadly lacking even in Europe. Greater Europe Mission did a survey in Paris and found 79 percent of the men and 24 percent of the women did not own a complete Bible. Bibles can be bought in bookstores in Western Europe, but they are expensive. There is an even greater shortage of Bibles in Eastern Europe and the Soviet Union where Communist governments try to hold down the circulation of God's Word. The executive secretary of the Bible

Society of Poland recently declared, "Instead of thousands of Bibles, we need millions." The problem in Poland is the shortage of paper.

For years I labored and prayed over the need for wider Bible distribution. I was especially concerned about the well-to-do and the leaders of countries such as my native India, who influence the masses as foreign missionaries can never do. I rarely saw a Bible when visiting government and business leaders. Many admitted to me they had never read a single verse. From talking to missionaries and national pastors, I learned that most Christian work was among poor people. Some told me, "If the rich people want Bibles, they can go to Christian bookstores." But I observed that Hindus and Muslims almost never go into Christian bookstores, apparently because of fear they will be identified as Christians.

Finally, the Lord gave me a plan. When I shared it with Dr. Richard Halverson, who is now chaplain of the United States Senate, he said, "Ro, the idea is so simple, only God could have thought of it."

Chapter 7

"Let Your Fingers Do the Walking"

WHEN I COMPLETED the translation of the Hmar New Testament, I rented a second floor office, just six-by-twelve feet, on Wheaton's Main Street. Partnership Mission was born.

"I am not 'antimissionary,'" I told the 114 friends on our first mailing list. "A missionary—Watkin Roberts—brought the gospel to our tribe. But then he had to go away, leaving the first Hmar believers to evangelize their own people, build their own churches, educate their own children.

"Thanks to Mr. Roberts and the Bible most members of our tribe are now Christians. We have hundreds of young men and women willing to go as missionaries themselves to other tribes. But we are poor and unable to train and send all of them.

"Remember, a national does not need passage money. He is already there. He does not need expensive equipment or language training. He speaks the language and is acquainted with the customs of the people. He cannot be expelled, for he is not a foreigner.

"So we ask for your financial partnership in our program

of nationals training and telling nationals. Ten dollars will pay the tuition of a Bible college student for one month; forty dollars will support a pastor or evangelist; one hundred dollars will operate an entire village school; one thousand dollars will build a two-room school."

My, how God blessed Partnership Mission. By our tenth anniversary, 1969, we could report 400 national missionaries, 135 churches, 65 village schools, a high school, and a hospital. But this was just one small corner of India.

One day I took a pencil and estimated how long it would take evangelical Christianity to reach all of India's then 500 million people (India has since grown to 700 million!). Based on the current rate of evangelization, and utilizing our total missionary effectiveness, I found that it would take 1,249 years to complete the task! "We cannot expect to live 1,249 years," I told Mawii.

I did a little more research and found that world population was growing by more than two persons per second, 132 per minute, 190,000 per day—more than a million and a quarter a week. By the end of 1969 there would be 67 million more people on earth.

I read that American churches owned $102 billion worth of real estate and would be spending a billion dollars on new church buildings, while contributions for world evangelization would amount to only $170 million. And I saw the pessimistic prediction of a leading Protestant educator that the organizational structure of the church would not make it to the end of the century.

The world picture was then looking very bleak. The United States was bogged down in Vietnam. Just the year before, six Christian and Missionary Alliance missionaries had been killed by Communist soldiers at Banmethuot, Vietnam. In 1964 and 1965 over 200 Catholic and Protestant missionaries had been killed by leftist revolutionaries.

The Holy Spirit kept nudging my mind with the Great

Commission of our Lord—"Go ye therefore, and teach all nations . . ." (Matt. 28:19). "And this gospel of the kingdom shall be preached in all the world for a witness unto all nations; and then shall the end come" (Matt. 24:14). The way the world was going, it seemed that the Lord's return would be the only answer. Was our Lord's return being delayed by the simple fact that the gospel had not yet been proclaimed to all nations?

The first American astronauts landed on the moon. How incredible that man now had the means to travel 240,000 miles into space, while on earth, after 2,000 years, most people still had not heard the Good News of God's everlasting love. Mawii and I and the children watched the moon-landing on television. We saw Neil Armstrong step from the space capsule and declare, "one small step for man, one giant leap for mankind." How many times as a boy in the jungle of northeastern India had I sat looking up at the moon, wondering what was really up there.

I had to laugh a little, thinking of what I was told as a boy back in Hmar country. Many Hmars actually believed there were two big banyan trees on the moonscape, with a monkey in one of the trees. They said that if you saw the monkey moving from one tree to the other, great fortune would come to your family. Oh, how I watched the moon.

Now I looked at the world and saw communism advancing and the free world shrinking. I read reports of Chinese claiming they had been healed of their diseases by looking to Mao Tse Tung. One young man testified that through constant repetition of the thoughts of Mao, he was now completely well and back at work.

A story about a postman in northeast China haunted me. It was said that he blazed a trail through an almost impenetrable forest to deliver mail to Communist production teams, stopping to carve the words, "Long live Chairman Mao!" on trees as he walked.

"Dear Lord," I prayed, "show me how to blaze new trails and get your Word out to the world."

About this time—January, 1970—a new challenge came from India. Friends from Hmar country wrote that the Communist member of parliament from my home state of Manipur had lost influence and could not be reelected. "Come and file as our candidate for parliament," they urged. "We can assure your election."

I showed Mawii the letter. She was flabbergasted. "Why, we'd have to give up our work here and return to India," she said.

"At least I can think and pray about it," I replied. "I gave up the dream of being a political leader years ago. Maybe the Lord is trying to tell me something now."

I prayed. I asked the opinion of my board members. The lights looked green all the way.

"Don't you see, Mawii, how this could advance the work of the mission?" I reasoned. "It would give it more status. I could involve the government in some of our projects. I could be a Christian witness on the floor of parliament. I could help other Christian groups working in India."

Mawii thought it would be a sidetrack. Nevertheless she knelt and prayed and asked the Lord to help her understand and be an encouragement to me.

When I left to catch my flight, she still had no peace. "I'll pray the Lord will give you peace about this decision as He has me," I promised as I stepped out of the car at the airport.

My flight was scheduled to arrive two days before the filing deadline—plenty of time, I thought, even if we were unexpectedly delayed somewhere enroute.

All went well until the plane landed for refueling at Tashkent on the southern tip of Russia. The pilot first announced we would be twenty-five minutes late taking off, then he said repairs had to be made and the passengers would have to go to a hotel.

It was twenty-five degrees below zero. The man assigned to share a room with me got drunk and vomited all over the bed. I shivered under the single blanket all night. The plane did not leave until the next afternoon and arrived fifteen minutes past the filing deadline.

The Hmar leaders had been camped at the New Delhi Airport, waiting for me. They were crushed when I arrived too late. I couldn't even talk until I tried to word a telegram to Mawii in the mission office. Finally, I told the Hmars, "Well, the Lord must have a purpose in this."

They had also planned for me to lead an evangelistic crusade in Imphal, a city with a population of half a million and yet without a single church. The Lord blessed the city in a marvelous fashion. Among the scores converted was a Muslim scholar. Before I left for America he told me of his intention to become a minister of Jesus.

Through spring and into that summer of 1970 I prayed and meditated. I thought of how the church had grown in my tribe, Hmars winning Hmars, then moving out to witness in adjoining tribes. How could we break through to the rest of India? What would be the best strategy?

Suddenly it seemed clear that India could only be evangelized by national leaders, teachers, lawyers, doctors, and government officials. But these were the very ones not being reached. It was known everywhere in India that Christianity had made its greatest inroads among the lowest castes. How often had I heard the upper class refer to these converts as "rice Christians."

The burden lingered. One warm autumn I was reflecting on how the gospel had come to our people. God had told one little British woman to send the Welsh missionary Watkin Roberts five pounds, about twenty-five American dollars. The missionary took that and printed the Gospel of John in the language of the tribe that adjoined the Hmars. Then he scattered those Gospels like seed throughout the area. The dear woman, who could not go to the mission field herself, gave the missionary money to buy seed—the Word of God. The missionary sowed that seed, and some of it fell among my people. It sprang up and bore much fruit. My family was part of that fruit.

"Lord, Your Word is the seed. But how do I spread it? How do I get it to the leaders?"

As I continued to pray, the telephone company jingle, "Let your fingers do the walking," broke my concentration. I couldn't stop thinking of it.

I gave up and got to my feet. My eyes caught two telephone directories on my desk. It was as if a voice shouted, "Here are the names and addresses of every person in New Delhi and Calcutta, the best educated, most influential people, the very ones you want to reach!"

"Thank You, Lord! Thank You! You've given me the idea. We can let our fingers do the walking. We can mail the New Testament to every person in the telephone directories of India. They won't reject it as foreign propaganda because it will be coming from one of their own.

"Maybe we can do it for the whole world. Somewhere there must be directories available for every country in the world. We can mail bright paperbacks to get the cost down. Books with colorful pictures.

"But why me, Lord? I'm only a little tribesman." The answer came back, "Because I chose you to be my messenger. Now go and obey."

I shared the idea with Mawii who was busy preparing our current newsletter. "Ro, it's wonderful," she declared.

A few days later Dr. Ken Taylor, the man who wrote *The Living Bible* paraphrase, dropped by. He wanted my opinion of a cover for a *Living New Testament* intended for Asian

EXTENT OF
BIBLE TRANSLATIONS
FOR ALL LANGUAGES

90% of known languages have the entire Bible
5% have the New Testament
3% have at least one book of the Bible
2% have no Scripture

distribution. I liked the title, *The Greatest Is Love*. But the cover showing a white man with a dark child on his back bothered me. "Asians won't like it," I told Ken. "They know whites don't go around carrying blacks on their back."

"Well, what would you suggest?" Ken asked.

I thought about it for a few moments while my friend was

drinking coffee. The Lord gave me the answer. "Use the Taj Mahal, Ken," I told him. "The Indian ruler Shah Jahan ordered this beautiful marble monument to be built in memory of his wife. It took 20,000 workmen twenty-one years to build it. The Taj is an Asian symbol of love."

Ken liked the idea. A couple of weeks later we were looking at the artist's version of the new cover. "It's beautiful, Ken," I said. "Asians will see the Taj and want to look inside the book."

Then I told him about the vision the Lord had given me of sending New Testaments to the leaders of India through the mail. "Could we use this same edition with the Taj cover?" I asked.

"Of course."

"Well, would we have to pay royalties for use of your *Living New Testament?*"

"To be given away? No."

"Could we put the Gospel of John first instead of Matthew? That way our new readers will immediately begin with the heart of the gospel message."

> Before anything else existed, there was Christ, with God. He has always been alive and is himself God. He created everything there is—nothing exists that he didn't make. Eternal life is in him, and this life gives light to all mankind. His life is the light that shines through the darkness—and the darkness can never extinguish it (John 1:1–5 TLB).

"Yes. If you think it best, Ro."

With this permission from Ken Taylor, I talked to his distributors for the Asian *Living New Testament*. They readily agreed to have the New Testaments for our test mailing printed at cost.

I began gathering information on the world telephone and postal systems. I already knew that Alexander Graham Bell invented the telephone. I hadn't known that the first telephone directory was printed in 1878, for New Haven, Connecticut, just two years after Bell demonstrated his newly patented invention at the American Centennial Exposition in Philadelphia. That first directory was only one page and included just six business listings. Now there were over 275 million.

We already had the telephone directories for Calcutta and New Delhi. We needed them for other cities in India and the rest of the world. I called the telephone company and was referred to Mr. Steve Allen, an executive with International Telephone and Telegraph in New York.

He was fascinated with what we wanted to do. "Getting the directories will be no problem," he assured me. "Except for the Soviet Union. We know the Russians publish directories for about 16 million subscribers, but they won't let us have them. When you get some," he laughed, "will you make copies for us?"

The telephone directories would tell us where to send Bibles. They would be delivered by "missionaries" from the post offices. I thought of the line, "Neither rain nor snow nor heat nor gloom of night stays these couriers from the swift completion of their appointed rounds." When I looked it up, I found it had been written by the Greek historian Herodotus about the Persian postal messengers of 500 B.C. Now God was going to use modern messengers of the mail to deliver his Word.

But could we mail Bibles to anywhere in the world where there were telephones? Would there be special restrictions and a variety of rates to the various countries?

Upon investigation, I found that a universal postal agreement had been in operation since July 1, 1875. This brought the signatory countries into a single postal territory for the exchange of mail at uniform postage rates.

The date 1875 immediately "rang a bell." Sure enough, that was the year Alexander Graham Bell sent the first sounds over a "telephone" wire, just twenty-nine days before the postal agreement was signed. What an interesting coincidence, or was it? Had God planned these two happenings for the same year, knowing that He would give us the idea for mailing Bibles almost a hundred years later?

The international headquarters of the Universal Postal Union is Berne, Switzerland. I immediately wrote them about our plan to mail Bibles. "Can I really mail a package from one post office to all other post offices in the world for the same amount of postage?" I asked.

"Yes, you can mail to every country in the world for the same price," the official assured me. "All you need are the addresses." He went on to explain that under the international agreement a package had to be delivered in the recipient country or returned to the sender with an explanation for why it could not be given to the addressee.

The man in Switzerland said there were more than 830,000 post offices, most of them open six days every week, with over four million postmen and postwomen knocking at doors. The sun never sets on the postal world. Regular delivery is going on somewhere every day of the week, because the Muslims have their sabbath on Friday, the Jews on Saturday, and the Christians on Sunday.

I called a meeting of our board, all Christian leaders in the Wheaton area, and explained the plan. "Say that again, Ro," one board member pressed.

I went over the idea again.

"Am I reading you right, Ro? You propose to mail a copy of the *Living New Testament* to everybody in India whose name and address is in the telephone directory. Then to Pakistan and Nepal and Thailand and on until you mail to the whole world? How much will this cost?"

"Well, at present rates, for printing and postage, we estimate it can be done for around a dollar each. The cost will likely go up before we are finished."

"And how many listings do you estimate there are in all the telephone directories?"

"Right now about 275 million. There will be more by the time we are done."

I could almost hear computers clicking in my board members' brains. "You're talking of 275 million dollars, at least," one noted.

"At least."

"And how much was our income for Partnership Mission last month?"

"I think it was about $25,000," I said.

The board talked some more. We prayed about it. Then they voted to begin. Later we changed our name to Bibles For The World!

We gave a print order for 50,000 copies and sent out an appeal to local churches for volunteers to come in and start typing labels, beginning with the Calcutta directory. People began responding.

I was so excited I could hardly eat or sleep. I envisioned a Buddhist mailman delivering the Word of God to another Buddhist, a Hindu handing the Book of the one true God to another Hindu, a Muslim taking the Bible to another Muslim, even a Communist delivering the Scriptures to a fellow Communist. What a great open door! The same God who said, "Cyrus, God's anointed," in the Old Testament would again be demonstrating his power in a worldwide manner (Is. 45:1 TLB).

I thought of how, as a youngster, Sadhu Sundar Singh was given a copy of the New Testament. The message troubled him so much that he tore up the book and threw away the pieces. Later he had second thoughts, retrieved the pieces, and put the book back together. Within a few hours he had received Christ as his Lord and Savior. Singh became India's greatest evangelist, traveling the world to win others to the Lord.

All the time I kept talking up the idea to whoever would listen. I took along a stack of copies to a Christian Businessmen's committee meeting. Holding up a New Testament with the beautiful color picture of the Taj Mahal on the cover, I said, "If you'll buy one like this for ten dollars I'll send nine more to India." I "sold" over thirty copies that way.

My joy over this response was reduced by a call from the printers. Since they were doing the job for cost, they had to have $10,000 to buy paper. "Within a week," the man said.

I put out the fleece. "Lord, if $10,000 comes in next week, we'll surely know you are behind this Bible mailing. I can't raise that much money by myself in so short a time."

On Sunday I shared the need with a small country church in Carlock, Illinois, where I was speaking. We had five minutes of silent prayer, asking God to provide. The money came in. If I had ever doubted, I was sure now that the Bible-mailing idea was from God.

The first shipment came from the printer. A swarm of volunteers helped address, package, and lick the mailing labels. Our most faithful worker was wheelchair-bound Carl Schingothe. "Maybe I can't walk," he laughed, "but I can serve the Lord by letting my fingers do the walking."

Each "love" gift of the New Testament contained a brief personal testimony from me and the invitation: "If you have any question or problem concerning Jesus Christ or on how you may have peace and everlasting life through Him, please write me." A return-address envelope was enclosed. We opened an office in New Delhi and waited prayerfully, expectantly for the first replies. What a thrill to receive a cablegram from our New Delhi representative: HUNDREDS OF LETTERS ARRIVING DAILY. FORWARDING SELECTIONS ON TO YOU.

A retired doctor wrote:

> I am greatly indebted to you for your kindness in sending me a copy of the Holy Bible in modern English, which I have read with pleasure and profit. For the last four years I have been looking anxiously forward to some reliable Holy Bible and approached two missionary societies doing house to house propaganda, but they could not supply my want. I had the pleasure of reading the Holy Bible as a textbook in my college days four decades hence [ago]. If you have any other publication relating to the life of Jesus Christ, kindly send to me.

Another letter bore an address in a wealthy part of Calcutta.

> Sir, I would like to know how you obtained my name and forwarded a copy of *The Best [Greatest] Is Love,* which I received through the post yesterday. It is with great delight that I shall read the New Testament.

A message from a man in the state of Haryana touched us.

> Thanks for the Bible in modern English. . . . In my town there is no church and other missionaries. So I cannot [ask] others about the Holy Father Christ.

Many other moving letters came telling of spiritual hunger.

> I finished the book sent by you. I was so moved by its eternal appeal that I couldn't restrain myself from writing a few lines to you. It is really the wisest book ever any human being read. I cannot just express how thankful I am to you for this wonderful book.

I do not find words with me to express my gratitude for *The Greatest Is Love*. Beliefs on concept of religion may differ from person to person—but the fact remains that without truth peace can't be achieved. Your book will help me find the way to "Right Faith, Right Knowledge, and Right Conduct."

I acknowledge *The Greatest Is Love* you sent me recently. . . . It is really good and marvelous. I want to read more literature. I am much interested to spread my knowledge in the Bible and also want to know the life of a Christian.

I have a religious bent of mind and have been reading several books on Hindu religion. . . . Although I started my school career in a Christian mission school and had read the Bible as a textbook, I could never develop the taste and admiration for the holy Christ as I have done from the text provided by you. I have hardly finished two chapters so far but could not restrain my desire of thanking you for the valuable gift which is almost a God-sent present to me at the opportune time.

Our first 50,000 mailing brought 20,000 letters with many writers requesting additional copies for friends. Many others wrote saying they had seen a copy of *The Greatest Is Love* at a friend's house and would like a copy of their own. These requests had not been expected, but our board voted to send them as long as funds permitted.

Our bank balance was dipping low when a Christian foundation offered to match every dollar given by others up to $250,000. The matching gifts were provided.

By Christmas, 1972, we were past the 300,000 mark for India with almost a million yet to mail. Still the letters kept coming, thousands and thousands. Never in my wildest dreams had I expected such an outpouring.

We began making plans to mail to other countries: 6,200

to Nepal; 162,000 to Burma; 62,000 to Sri Lanka; 165 to tiny Bhutan; and 250 to Sikkim.

A pastor in Ohio asked if his family could take Sikkim with its 250 telephone listings as their Christmas present to the Lord. His children were willing to give up some presents so that the leaders of Sikkim might have God's Word. We mailed them the books and labels. The parents typed the addresses, and the four children helped pack and apply the labels and stamps. Then after delivering the Bibles to the post office, they knelt and prayed that the Lord would use their love gift.

After mailing almost a half a million to India, Mawii and I could wait no longer to return home and see firsthand how the mailing was being received. It was more than I had anticipated. I saw *The Greatest Is Love* almost everywhere I went—in the hotel lobby, in the post office, and even in the bank where I went to exchange some money.

The New Testament was lying on the bank manager's desk. "Where did you get this beautiful book?" I asked.

"Oh, I got it in the mail and have just begun to read it. I don't know who sent it or how he got my name."

"Well, I'm happy to tell you that I am the president of the organization that sent it."

He was impressed and pleased.

I took a flight to Calcutta and as I walked down the aisle of the big Boeing jet I saw a familiar face engrossed in one of the books. There was a vacant seat beside him, and I asked if I could sit down. "Certainly," he said.

"Oh, by the way, what book are you reading?"

He looked at the cover and said, "It's called *The Greatest Is Love.*"

"How did you get that book?"

"It came by mail quite a few weeks ago, but I never had the time to read it. I told my wife to tuck it in my briefcase, and I would read it on my next trip."

"Do you know who sent it?"

He flipped back the first two pages and saw the pencil drawing of my face. "You are the one?"

"Yes, I happen to be the one, and I'm glad you are reading it."

He told me he had once been the Indian ambassador to Washington and after that a cabinet member. Now he was the chief justice of the Supreme Court of India. Of course, I already knew that.

"Do you know," he continued, "that while I was an ambassador in America I had a secret longing to read the Bible through at least once while I was out of the country? But I never owned one. I would see one once in a while in a hotel room, but I didn't think I should take it away. I could have bought one in a Christian bookstore, but I didn't feel I should go there. When this book came, I saw it as the fulfillment of my desire, so I asked my wife to save it for a time when I could read it."

Then he said, "If I have any questions or problems, could I get in touch with you?"

"Of course," I assured him. "I would be honored to hear from you. My address is in the front of your Bible."

Because of the excitement created by the arrival of two truckloads of Bibles just prior to my own arrival in New Delhi, I was swamped by reporters requesting interviews. I didn't know what to do. Finally, my good friend Mr. V. V. Purie, a leading Indian businessman, arranged a press conference for me at the Intercontinental Hotel and invited the newspapers and broadcast stations to send representatives. A large number of curious reporters came to meet the former tribesman who had been mailing Bibles all over India.

After everyone else had asked questions, the reporter for the *Hindustan Standard,* one of the largest newspapers in India, said very courteously, "Do I have my information right, sir, that you hope to mail a Bible to every telephone subscriber in the world, and there are now over 300 million people in the phone books around the world?"

"Yes, that is correct. When we started there were only 275 million. The total now is around 300 million."

"And you have phone books from all these countries?"

"Either we have them, or we can get them."

"Will you then be mailing to Russia?"

"Yes," I finally said, "but right now the door isn't open so we can't mail there."

The reporter for the *Indian Express* popped up. "Mr. Pudaite, do you know about the cultural agreement signed between India and Russia just two years ago? It provides for each country to send books to the other. Since you are an Indian and the Bible is your cultural book, why not send Bibles under that agreement?"

"Well, I didn't know about that agreement," I said in surprise.

"Go to the Soviet Embassy," the reporter proposed. "Show them your book. Ask if they will let you mail under the agreement. If they say no, call another press conference and tell us."

I called the embassy and asked for an appointment. "Yes, I'll be glad to see you tomorrow at ten," the cultural attaché said.

When I walked in the next morning, they received me like royalty. I had hardly given my name to the secretary when the cultural attaché, a huge bear of a man, came rushing from his office, arms extended, shouting, *"Russie, Hindi, bhai! bhai!"* ("Russians and Indians are brothers!")

I didn't know what to do except hold out my short arms and say, "Yes—*Hindi, Russie, bhai, bhai!*" He was so big I couldn't get my arms halfway around him.

"Come into my office, my friend, and tell me what you need," he said, leading the way.

I had hardly begun, when he interrupted. "Yes, yes, I know the whole story. One of our reporters was at your press conference."

"Then can we mail Bibles into Russia?"

"Of course. But you must help me by please accepting certain conditions."

"What do you wish?"

"Number one, you will please print from a Bible that has already been published inside Russia so the customs will not stop it. Number two, you will please print in India. And number three, you will please mail from India."

"That will be no problem," I assured him. "How many may we mail?"

"Ten thousand a month. If you mail more, we might have difficulties."

I left, eager to find an Indian printer. But first there was an engagement to keep. I had rented the well-known Sapru House auditorium and placed ads in New Delhi's two biggest newspapers, inviting those who had received *The Greatest Is Love* in the mail to come at seven the following evening and "hear the life story of the man who sent you this book."

As the time drew near for the meeting, I paced up and down in our hotel room. "What if no one shows up?" I told Mawii. "What if we didn't do enough?"

I needn't have been concerned. Ninety minutes before the meeting was to start, the auditorium manager called excitedly. "Please come now," he urged. "The building is already packed and we're turning people away."

We hurried over. Because my voice was beginning to tire, I asked Mawii to give her testimony first. Then the Lord restored my voice, and I spoke for forty or fifty minutes, telling what God had done through the Bible in our tribe. Finally—and huskily—I said, "I cannot talk any longer. If any one of you wishes to speak with us about believing in

Jesus Christ, then please come to the front and we will try to help you."

No one moved for a second or two; then it was like a wall that started forward. At least half the audience wanted to come. "My friends," I said, "so many are wanting to come it is impossible to see you all. Could you please call our office and make appointments? Here is our telephone number."

The phone never stopped ringing the next day.

Before leaving New Delhi for a nostalgic visit to Hmar country, I met again with Mr. Purie who owns and operates one of the largest printing presses in Asia. I told him about the Russian opportunity and said, "If you can help us get a Russian Bible and the telephone directories, I'll give you the printing orders."

"How many telephone subscribers are there in Russia?" he asked.

"Sixteen million," I replied, quoting the figure given to me by Steve Allen, the telephone company executive in New York. "But right now we can only send ten thousand a month."

Mr. Purie smiled. "That will be sufficient to send a man to Moscow."

The Hindu printer sent his Hindu associate to a Communist country for the cause of the Bible. He returned with the Moscow telephone directory, which the man at IT&T had been unable to get. Within a short time we were mailing Bibles inside the Soviet Union.

The years hurried by. The mailings continued. We built a new headquarters and enlarged our staff. We experimented with new covers and titles. We printed in new languages. The New Testament went out. The letters came back—thousands and thousands and thousands.

A professor in Pakistan found one of the New Testaments at his college library. "I am a Muslim believing in all the prophets from Adam to Muhammed. . . . Please send me the Holy Book in English or Urdu and also books on Christianity."

A secretary in Kenya reported she had opened the Bible sent to her boss. "I am very much interested to know about the supernatural power, greatest love, Jesus Christ, the truth and the life," she wrote. "I should be most grateful if you would kindly post me a Bible."

From Malaysia: "I was filled with great joy when I saw your book. . . . I am slowly stepping into the world of Christianity."

From Bermuda, the wife of the managing director of an internationally known insurance company said that her husband had found *The Greatest Is Love* on his desk. Thinking it a novel meant for her, he took it home. She wrote in appreciation:

> It certainly was intended for me, as I was, at the time, a nonbeliever. Soon, however, I became fascinated by the Greatest Love Story of all time. I now write, as a growing Christian, confident in the strength of My Lord and Savior Jesus Christ, and today during my prayer time, He reminded me that I should write to thank you. I do so sincerely, for the important part you played in bringing me before the throne of grace.

God supplied the money needed to print and mail millions of Bibles. We received a few large gifts, but most donations were from ten to one hundred dollars. A blind man gave twenty dollars. A faithful doctor sent money from his pension fund. A dear woman gave one hundred dollars that had been set aside for a new stereo. After she mailed the check, someone gave her family a stereo. Senior citizens mailed offerings from their pension checks. Children sent coins from piggy banks.

Christian celebrities helped us with big rallies. Pat and

Shirley Boone, two of our most loyal and devoted friends, headlined a meeting at Auburn University in Alabama that was attended by the governor, lieutenant governor, a future governor, and Miss Alabama. Alabamans sent Bibles to Bangladesh.

Our dear brother Doug Oldham sang for a Bibles For The World rally in the Pickard Civic Auditorium of little Neenah, Wisconsin. Some of the overflow watched on closed circuit TV. Others had to be turned away. Led by Reverend Elden Davis, pastor of the local Calvary Bible Church, the people of Neenah provided Bibles for every telephone subscriber in Afghanistan. We didn't know then that Afghanistan would soon be taken over by the Soviet army.

Even with postage rates rising, the Bibles kept going out. From 1971 to 1981 we mailed seven million copies, including 500,000 to the Soviet Union.

The letters continued coming. One of our national evangelists wrote that an entire Burmese family had become Christians through reading one of the New Testaments we mailed. A gentleman from Hong Kong said, "My house has never seen a Bible before today. From now on I will thank God for this New Testament in Chinese that you have kindly and freely mailed me."

Our representative in Taiwan reported that a young man called him and told him he had been depressed about life and planning to commit suicide. As he was on his way to take his own life, he saw a copy of the Chinese New Testament we had sent lying on a bus. He picked up the book and began to read. Instead of lying on the railroad track to be run over by a train, he read the Scripture and confessed his sins to God.

The wife of a businessman in Zimbabwe wrote that her husband was at his sports' club when he noticed a copy of the book on the manager's desk. When the manager said he had no use for it, the businessman asked if he could take it home. "That was one month ago," the businessman's wife wrote. "My husband has given his life to God. I do feel this Bible had a lot to do with it as Trevor could understand what he was reading. On behalf of my children and myself we thank you for your love in sharing God with others." She added a P.S. "Will you send a copy to two friends who went to church for the first time with us last Sunday?"

One of the most thrilling stories came from our friend Ed Lacaba who told about meeting a dynamic new Christian from the Philippines at a prayer breakfast in Los Angeles. The Filipino, a wealthy real estate broker named Tony Isit, had told the group: "I am a believer in Jesus Christ because an Indian man sent me a Bible from Illinois. I got so excited about God's Word, after finding a copy in my mail box, that I bought all the Bibles I could find and gave them to friends and neighbors. At my Bible studies and prayer groups, more than 500 people have accepted Jesus Christ as Savior."

After the breakfast, Ed got to Tony Isit fast. "Is the 'Indian man in Illinois' who sent you the Bible named Ro?"

"No, it's a longer name than that," Tony told him.

"Is it Rochunga Pudaite?" Ed asked.

"Yes, that's the one. Do you happen to know him?"

"I certainly do," Ed responded and related how he had met me in Wheaton five years earlier.

When Ed contacted us, I lost no time in getting in touch with this remarkable Filipino. I finally reached him by telephone in Las Vegas where he was arranging a real estate transaction for a client.

"Am I really talking to the person who made all that difference in my life?" Tony asked in amazement after I introduced myself. "Are you really the one who sent me the Bible?"

"Well," I said, "I head an organization that sends millions of Bibles overseas through the mail, so a lot of people worked together to send you that New Testament. All of us thank God it got to you safely."

"Mr. Pudaite," Tony continued, "though I am only thirty-five years old, I've been very successful in business. But I didn't know how to live with that success, and I was just about ready to give it all up when that book showed up in my mailbox. In fact, I have three homes in the Philippines, and on the same day a Bible arrived at each of those homes, and I got all three of them. I couldn't help saying to myself, 'There must be a reason for someone sending me three copies of this book, so I must read it.'

"I came to where it said, 'Except a man be born again, he cannot see the kingdom of God' [John 3:3]. That statement went round and round in my mind for a long time, and then I just prayed, 'Lord Jesus, I can't solve it for myself. Come into my heart and take over my life.' That is the way it happened to me."

Tony became a one-man Bibles-for-the-Philippines operation. He has given out Bibles to thousands of people.

We didn't print the story of the Russian mailing in our newsletter for a long time. When we did mention it, people began immediately asking, "Are your Bibles really getting into Russia? Are you sure they aren't being intercepted at the post office and confiscated before they can reach the people?"

We wanted to be very cautious in following up, because the Bibles were continuing to go out at the rate of 10,000 a month. But on a trip into Russia for us, Dr. Cliff Robinson found evidence in a most unusual way.

He and his party were in a city some 2,000 miles south of Moscow. Their official interpreter had helped them find Christian leaders and churches and worked tirelessly in their behalf. One day Cliff said to her, "We do so appreciate your good work and would like to reward you with a small bonus."

"Oh, no, I wouldn't think of it. This has been a totally new experience for me. I was never in a Christian church before, and I have learned many new things."

"But isn't there something I can do for you or get for you—just as a friend?" Cliff insisted.

She repeated Cliff's words "as a friend" aloud. Then she said, "You are 'Bibles For The World'—right? Do you print anything besides the Bible?"

When Cliff said we did not, she asked, "But what about the *Evangelische?*"

Cliff didn't understand so he asked her what the book was about.

"Oh, it is all about Jesus Christ and what He taught. I especially liked His statement that we are not to judge lest we also be judged. And He said if you are slapped on one side of the face to turn the other side also. If we did that, there certainly would be no war. There must be two to fight." As Cliff listened, she told him other bits and pieces from the Sermon on the Mount.

"Tell me about this *Evangelische*," Cliff said excitedly. "Was there a picture of the Cathedral in the Kremlin on the cover?"

"I don't know," she told Cliff, "since I've never been to Moscow. But there was a building with yellow towers—it could have been a church."

Cliff could hardly believe his ears. She was talking about the very book Bibles For The World had been sending into Russia for several months. But how could she have gotten the book far to the south of Moscow? All of our mailings up to this time had been in the Moscow area. Cliff asked her to tell him more.

"A friend from Moscow visited here recently," she explained, "and showed me the book she had received through the mail. I found it exciting and asked if she would lend it to me. I had it all to myself for two days before giving it back."

"Do you mean," Cliff said, "that what you told me about Jesus was what you learned from reading the New Testament for just two days?" he asked her in amazement.

"Yes," she replied, "I was very sad when my friend took back her book and returned to Moscow. But you said you wanted to do something for me as a friend. Do you think you could get me a copy of the New Testament for my own?"

Cliff and his wife Betty had already given their personal Bibles away. That night when he told the story to their group, one of the members, Phyllis Weaver, offered her leather bound Testament in English. When Cliff presented this *"Evangelische"* to the interpreter, she burst into tears and sobbed, "Thank you! Thank you!" Then she went directly to Phyllis Weaver and thanked her profusely before all the others.

Cliff passed the thrilling story along to us. We immediately sent her a Russian New Testament through our New Delhi office.

A few months after this unusual experience, Cliff met three Russian evangelical leaders at the Washington airport and escorted them to the National Prayer Breakfast. At the prayer breakfast one of the group, Dr. Ilia Orlov, a medical doctor and dentist as well as an ordained minister, praised Bibles For The World before the large audience, which included President Carter, many U.S. senators and representatives, Chief Justice Warren Burger, foreign ambassadors, and many other dignitaries. He said:

> The Word of God is needed all over the world, but especially do the people of my country love the Bible. I know that God's Word will not return unto Him void, but it always

accomplishes the divine purpose. We are so thankful for the vision of Bibles For The World, for it is sowing the seed of the Word all over the world.

Many thousands of my compatriots are receiving Bibles today because of these beautiful Christian brothers and their ambitious program to send the Bible to everybody listed in the telephone books of the world. We know that God's Word is not bound, and it cannot be! We are grateful to be a part of this program. We wear the logo pin of Bibles For The World, not only on our coat lapels, but even more proudly carry its banner in our hearts.

After all this publicity, I asked our New Delhi printer if Russian officials there were showing any concern about the continued mailings of Bibles into Russia. "They frequently visit my plant, for we do some work for them," he said. "Not only do they raise no objection about the mailings, but they usually ask for a copy of the Bible, which we are happy to give them."

Chapter 8

My Billion Bible Dream

BIBLES, BIBLES, BIBLES. Bibles everywhere in our offices. Volunteers typing address labels from the world's telephone directories. Others packing Bibles and trucking them to the post office. Thousands of letters bearing canceled exotic postage stamps coming back from grateful recipients, overflowing cardboard boxes. Other volunteers sorting through the letters, writing letters of personal response to seekers abroad.

To India, Burma, Pakistan, Afghanistan, Bhutan, Bangladesh, Nepal, Sri Lanka, Thailand, Malaysia, Hong Kong, Taiwan, Singapore, Japan, Korea, Indonesia, the Philippines, Kenya, Zimbabwe, Jamaica, Bermuda, South Africa, Guyana, Ireland, and many other countries went Bibles during the hectic seventies. We were mailing so many Bibles—over six million—and handling so much correspondence that we had to enlarge our offices four times. Mission executives forwarded requests for Bibles and asked us to supply desperately needed Bibles all over the world.

Yet every time I looked at the size of the latest telephone directories I became overwhelmed. When we started in

1971 there were 275 million phone listings in the directories of the world. The number of listings increased much faster than our Bible-mailings. By 1980 there were 520 million names and addresses. This was an increase of 245 million since we started, over forty times the mailings we had made.

I looked at our devoted staff—so busy, so hard-working—many of them retired folks who were giving their services, all so caught up in the excitement of sharing God's Word with the world. I looked at Mawii laboring through a stack of correspondence, answering the telephone that never seemed to stop ringing, often going home to fix dinner for the children, then returning to work at her desk late into the night. I looked at my schedule with so many speaking engagements ahead and wondered how I would be able to meet every date.

Meanwhile our bookkeeping manager said the cost of paper and printing was going up again. Another postage increase was predicted soon. Inflation was pounding at our heels.

When I mentioned inflation to a missionary leader, he said, "You don't have to tell me, Ro. It's costing us nearly $40,000 a year to keep a missionary couple in Japan."

Then I saw a prediction that made my hair almost stand on end. By 1990—just a decade away—there would be over a billion telephones in the world. A billion addresses to mail God's Word to. A billion stops for "missionary" postal workers. A billion opportunities to obey God's command, "Go ye into all the world . . ." (Mark 16:15). A billion telephone addresses representing a billion homes with five billion people!

A billion opportunities! Our goal was to mail only one million Bibles the next year.

Was mailing the Bible to everybody in the world's telephone directories really an impossible dream? Could the world wait 500 years to get Bibles at the rate we were going, allowing for no further growth in the telephone subscriber population?

I shared this burden with some friends and one suggested, "Why not be content, Ro, with the ministry God has given you?"

"How can I be content," I replied, "when God has called us to reach the world with His Word?"

Yet, secretly, I became discouraged. When the money didn't come in for the printing, we had to ask the printer to wait. It was always, "Shall we go ahead with the next country, or shall we wait until all the money is in to pay for the printing?"

I felt frustrated.

I looked again at statistics on Bible distribution. Eighty-five percent of the estimated 2.1 billion Bibles printed since Gutenberg were in English. Eighty-five percent for only nine percent of the world's people.

The great majority of new telephone subscribers were non-English speaking.

I did some figuring. It was now costing us $2.40 to print, package, and mail a Bible—including office overhead and staff salaries. Soon the cost would be more than $2.50.

Where would we find over two-and-one-half billion dollars to mail one billion Bibles?

I looked at a table of national expenditures in the United States. Next year this country would be spending $135,600,000,000 on national defense, up from $98,031,451,000 the previous year. Down the page my eye caught another figure. American churches had invested nearly $4 billion in new church construction during the past year.

If God's people could give that much in one year for sanctuaries and Sunday school classrooms, why couldn't we raise two billion plus dollars in ten years to help fulfill the Great Commission and hasten the return of Christ?

BIBLES FOR THE WORLD MAILED 6,444,62

(Countries are identified by numeral

1–India 1,300,000	12–Cyprus 5,000
2–Nepal 10,000	13–Afganistan 32,000
3–Bhutan 287	14–Philippines 468,392
4–Bangladesh 110,000	15–Iran 50,000
5–Burma 29,000	16–Taiwan 1,574,530
6–Singapore 161,000	17–Hong Kong 230,000
7–Malaysia 150,000	18–Macao 40,000
8–Thailand 210,000	19–Indonesia 17,000
9–Sri Lanka 85,000	20–North Ireland 28,000
10–Pakistan 211,000	21–Kenya 48,387
11–U.S.S.R. 600,000	22–South Korea 200,000

NEW TESTAMENTS FROM 1971–1982.
followed by number of Bibles mailed.)

23–Japan 235,000
24–China 30,000
25–Bermuda 17,580
26–South Africa 225,000
27–Zimbabwe 58,000
28–Guyana 20,000
29–Ghana 1,000
30–Guam 4,000
31–Jamaica 40,000
32–Nigeria 500
33–Tanzania 15,000

34–Virgin Islands 2,000
35–Carolina Islands 1,000
36–Zambia 8,000
37–Haiti 1,000
38–Puerto Rico 1,000

Other African countries 200,000
Miscellaneous 4,000
USA disabled veterans 20,000
USA foreign embassies 1,952

I chuckled, remembering what my dear old father had said when I first told him we were going to mail everybody listed in telephone directories a Bible to let the whole world read God's Word. "My son, God has given you the idea for all of us to go to heaven alive."

"What do you mean, my Father?" I asked.

"Our Lord said in Matthew 24:14, 'And this gospel of the kingdom shall be preached in all the world for a witness unto all nations; and then shall the end come.'

"When you drop the last Bible in the mail, I'll listen for the trumpet of God. Go and do your job in a hurry. I don't want to be dead and buried. I want to be alive and caught up to meet the Lord."

I smiled as I thought of the simple faith of my dear Father, now eighty-seven years old.

Then I realized that at the rate we and all other Bible distributors—indeed, the whole Body of Christ—were going, he would be disappointed. The job wouldn't even be finished in my lifetime.

"Lord, how can we climb this mountain? It is higher and steeper than I ever thought it would be. And how can we stir up the entire Body of Christ to go forth and fulfill the Great Commission in this generation?"

My discouragement lingered. I would rise early in the morning to pray and pour out my heart to the Lord. "How can we climb this mountain?" I kept imploring.

"My child," the Lord reminded, "haven't I always provided for you? You have only to give yourself completely to me. Do you remember that time in Calcutta when you gave all you had and I provided?"

I remembered. It was at the beginning of the college year in Calcutta. I had all my scholarship money in my wallet, about 350 rupees, then worth about 85 American dollars. I was in the Carey Baptist Church listening to Mrs. W. C. Bowker tell about the need for the printing of the Tibetan

Bible. The Bible had been translated before World War II and kept hidden during the war. Now it could be printed, she said, but there was not enough money.

Pastor Walter Corlett called two students to the front to take the offering. "I don't want Mrs. Bowker going to another church," he said. "Please give a very generous offering so the Tibetan Bible can be printed."

My heart said, "Give all the money in your wallet." My head said, "What will you do for the next three months? Ten rupees is all you can spare."

I was struggling so much that the offering plate passed and I didn't even see it. Didn't give a rupee. Then Pastor Corlett spoke again. "Well, I hope you have given all you could. But just in case there are some who want to give more or might not have given and would like to pray about it some more, I'm going to put a basket at the door."

My heart won over my head. I put all I had in the basket, including the change in my pocket. Afterward, I watched my friends hop on the street car for the ride back to school, while I had to walk the five miles because I had given even my pocket change. When I got to the school, the gate was closed. The guard had to come and open it for me. I was embarrassed to be late.

That night I didn't sleep well. My head kept saying, "Why did you have to give all you had? What will you do now for your school expenses?"

The next morning a man handed me a plain white envelope on which was written simply "Rochunga." I opened it and there was one hundred rupees. No note or inscription. Just one hundred beautiful rupees, inserted between a folded white paper. I cried and prayed, "Thank you, Lord, You are so faithful. I will never doubt You again. Now please help me stretch this money for the whole three months." And He did. Through careful budgeting I never went hungry a single day.

"Now," the Lord said, "*abide in Me*. If I could provide for you then, why will I not now?"

When I told Mawii, she reminded me of Campbell Morgan's rendering of John 15:7: "If you abide in Me and My words abide in you, you shall *demand as your due* whatever you are inclined to, and it shall be generated unto you." I breathed a sigh of relief.

Still I could not fully comprehend. I wanted to see, and I could not visualize how we could possibly raise 2.4 billion dollars, the amount now projected for mailing a billion Bibles.

Maybe it was because contributions dropped off sharply that month and we had to hold our mailings back. Maybe it was because I became so tired from trying to speak in so many churches so far apart. Whatever the reason, the door of my heart swung open for Satan to feed my doubting spirit. Even my beloved Mawii, who almost always is the one to lift me up, became somewhat apprehensive. For several days we moped about the house and office. We were both so down in the dumps.

Then one morning Mawii called, "Ro, come here! Listen to these verses."

She read from the small soft-bound *Living Bible* I had given her a little while after we started the mailings. "Ro, it says, 'Rest in the Lord; wait patiently for him to act. . . . Don't fret and worry—it only leads to harm' (Ps. 37:7,8).

"Ro, we don't have to worry. We don't have to bear the burden ourselves. We can just 'rest in the Lord' and 'wait patiently for Him to act.' Isn't that wonderful?

"Ro, dear Ro, do you remember the promise the Lord gave me when we first began the Bibles For The World program? When such a heavy responsibility was placed upon me for which I felt I had neither the training, experience, nor ability. After days of heart searching, the Lord spoke to me from Psalm 32:8: 'I will instruct you . . . and guide you along the best pathway for your life; I will advise you and watch your progress' (TLB). Ro, He is guiding and instructing us day by day as we go to Him for every big and little problem. His counsel will come to you. He is watching how we make progress even as we follow the guidance He gives us day by day."

I read Mawii's verses aloud. I read them again. "Ah, Mawii, how could I have been so ignorant? How could I forget that the Lord will supply our every need? Mawii, I have been thinking too much of what we can do and not enough of what God can do as we trust Him."

What a beautiful prayer fellowship we enjoyed together. Satan had been rebuked by the Word of God. How ironic, I thought. Here I had been devoting all my energies to giving *others* the Word of God and I did not use this Sword of the Spirit to fight off the attacks of Satan. How could I have been so blind as to forget the example of our Lord in answering Satan's temptations: "It is written . . ." (Matt. 4:1–11)?

Shortly thereafter the Lord gave Mawii some new directions. As is her custom when faced with problems larger than her share, she went straight to the Lord.

This secret of strength and habit was formed from a life of deprivation. Here in America we are blessed with so many Christian "how to" books and countless ministers and mature, godly Christians. We can quickly find an answer to almost every problem, and to some problems we never knew existed.

Mawii did not have these privileges when we were growing up. We had almost no one but the Lord in which to confide and almost no book beside the Bible from which to seek counsel. And from Him and His Word Mawii receives her sustenance and guidance.

One Sunday evening, as she prayed and pondered about the schedule of the coming week, she was filled with fear and anxiety and, most of all, overwhelmed with a sense of inadequacy. That evening the Lord gave her His words in 1 Chronicles 28:19–21 to strengthen her heart to face the week.

She shared these new directions when we asked her to open our board meeting with a brief devotional message. Afterward I went back and read with new insight the instruction and encouragement that King David gave Solomon for building the temple. "Every part of this blueprint," he told his son, "was given to me in writing from the hand of the Lord" (1 Chr. 28:19 TLB). "Every part of this blueprint," I repeated.

"But, Lord," I pleaded, "David was a mighty king with a whole nation behind him, and we are such a small organization. We are so few and the mission so enormous."

The Lord then brought to my mind the time when Jethro saw that Moses was trying to meet all of the needs of the children of Israel by himself. I turned back to Exodus to read what Jethro had told his son-in-law:

> You're going to wear yourself out—and if you do, what will happen to the people? Moses, this job is too heavy a burden for you to try to handle all by yourself. Now listen, and let me give you a word of advice, and God will bless you . . . Find some capable, godly, honest men who hate bribes, and appoint them as judges, one judge for each 1000 people; he in turn will have ten judges under him, each in charge of a hundred; and under each of them will be two judges, each responsible for the affairs of fifty people; and each of these will have five judges beneath him, each counseling ten persons. Let these men be responsible to serve the people with justice at all times. Anything that is too important or complicated can be brought to you. But the smaller matters they can take care of themselves . . . (Ex. 18:18–22, TLB).

"If we can't do it all ourselves," I told Mawii, "we can follow the Jethro principle."

Dear Mawii smiled ever so softly, as if she had known this from God all the time.

I flipped back to the chapter in 1 Chronicles where David told Solomon, "Be strong and courageous and get to work. Don't be frightened by the size of the task. . . . He will see to it that everything is finished correctly" (28:20 TLB).

My heart was getting stronger. My faith was expanding. How many times had I said in counseling others, "Faith is like a rubber band. The more you stretch it, the further it will reach." God was applying that analogy afresh to me.

Oh, how my heart leaped when I saw the next verse: "And these various groups of priests and Levites will serve in the Temple. Others with skills of every kind will volunteer, and the army and the entire nation are at your command" (v. 21).

I wanted to leap and dance about, but I didn't for I feared my children might think their father had gone crazy.

A scene from my trip to India for the peace mission with the tribal rebels flashed before my memory. I saw two mail trucks being escorted by army vehicles in front and behind to the capital of the state of Mizoram. The nation of India was making sure that the mail was not intercepted.

Entire nations were at our command. When we mailed Bibles, they guaranteed that the postal carriers would deliver the precious copies of God's Word to the people listed in the telephone books.

"But the money, Lord?" I asked again. "We may find enough people to help us, but where will we get over two billion dollars to mail a billion Bibles?"

The Lord assured my heart from 1 Chronicles 29, which lists all the resources David promised Solomon. David knew that the young crown prince was about to tackle a big job. He also realized that Solomon would be frightened by the mountain before him—the task, the cost, the workers needed to build the temple.

As an expression of his devotion to the temple of His God, David personally donated 3,000 talents of pure gold from Ophir and 7,000 talents of refined silver (v. 4). *The Living Bible* puts these amounts in dollars, $85,000,000 worth of gold and $20,000,000 worth of silver. I knew the price of these precious metals had gone way up since Dr. Ken Taylor did his translation. I checked a Bible dictionary and calculated that 3,000 talents of pure gold would be about 110 tons or almost 4 million ounces. I looked to see what the market price of gold was that day on the London market. Four million ounces would bring exactly $2.4 billion!

I was floored. I just cried out and said, "Lord, thank you. If David could give $2,400,000,000 in gold for the temple, surely You can lead us to faithful people who will donate that much to complete the Bible task by 1990."

As I read on, I was overwhelmed. With King David leading the way, the clan leaders, the heads of the tribes, the army officers, and the administrative officers came bringing enormous sums for the building of the temple. I said, "Lord, if you were willing to provide such resources for building a temple of rocks and mortar that can be destroyed, how much more will you give us the resources to build Your temple in the hearts of millions of people in every nation—a temple, not made with hands, which will last forever."

Soon after this I shared what God had given me with about a hundred people at a retreat. "How many of you," I asked, "would be willing to give $1,000 for the billion Bible dream God has given us." Eighteen people said they would.

I presented the challenge to a church in Maryland. Four members said they would give at least $1,000. The dear pastor stepped forward and said he was going to pray that the church would give at least $100,000.

I showed a church in Minnesota how simple it was to mail

a Bible. Taking out the wrapper a manufacturer had developed for us, I said, "You don't need to worry with tape or staples. You don't have to lick anything and get germs on your tongue. You just slip the New Testament inside the wrapper, fold over the sides, press the middle, and squeeze the ends. Like this. Then you stick on the address label and affix the postage, which now is only eighty-three cents for anywhere in the world. Then take it to the post office or mailbox."

The church gave an offering that morning to mail 5,000 Bibles.

At still another church I presented the idea of mailing a Bible a day from each home. "Let your children see where the Bibles are going. Let members of the family take turns wrapping and putting the labels on. Father can take Sunday; mother, Monday; brother, Tuesday; and sister, Wednesday. You may read a passage from the book before wrapping. Then start all over again."

There was a wonderful response.

The Lord gave us another idea. We "sell" individual Christians, Sunday school classes, Bible study groups, and churches a carton of fifty Bibles with mailing labels, wrappers, and mailing instructions. All of the Bibles can be taken to the post office at one time, or a certain number can be mailed every day or week.

"We can arrange for you to receive letters from recipients so you can see the result of your involvement in world missions," we tell people who might be interested in this project.

Every approach we take brings wonderful responses. When I present the billion Bible challenge, I always say, "If you can find a better way to send the Word of God to the world, then please come and tell us or do it yourself."

I always emphasize that the field is the world, the seed is the Word of God, the harvest is the end of the world, and the reapers are the angels—the messengers of the Good News. "The missionaries and national workers cannot reap where the seed has not been sown," I remind. "Remember the Ethiopian eunuch! He read the Bible and *then* God sent Philip to interpret for him. He became a believer and was baptized."

As we moved into 1981 the excitement increased. God gave us a simple plan. We asked the Lord for a director to find and train hundreds who would give the challenge and invite churches, Sunday school classes, home Bible studies, families, and individuals to join us in fulfilling the billion Bible dream.

God provided the director from among the thousands touched by Bible mailings. The postman delivered a Bibles For The World New Testament to Alwyn Zoutendijk's office address, as listed in the telephone directory of Bermuda. A top insurance executive in South Africa, Alwyn had just been appointed the corporate manager of his company's international office in Bermuda. He glanced at the cover of the book titled *The Greatest is Love* and told his secretary. "Somebody must have sent me a novel. I'll take it home for my wife to read."

Alwyn didn't know that his wife Lisa was spiritually searching. Through reading *The Greatest Is Love* she came to know Christ as her personal Savior. Her transformed life was such a powerful witness to Alwyn that he made a spiritual recommitment. Both became active in a local church and began teaching Sunday school.

Mawii and I later met Alwyn and Lisa at a retreat in Bermuda. Both immediately became excited about the billion Bible dream. Soon we were discussing plans for the future, along with Alwyn and Lisa's desire to discover the will of God for their lives.

Five months later they joined our staff and moved to Wheaton. Now, under Alwyn's leadership, we are gathering a team of missionaries who will work toward the fulfillment of the billion Bible dream. Lisa is wholeheartedly involved with a force of volunteers who write letters of counsel and spiritual instruction to the thousands of persons responding to the Bible mailing.

We are so thrilled at the opportunity God has placed before us and His church. God, we believe, is going to enable us to mail a billion Bibles. A billion copies of the Book that transformed many people from a backward, primitive, headhunting tribe to a model of moral and spiritual development and material progress. A billion copies of this Book that God inspired and has preserved through the ages, this Book that speaks to the heart of all humanity, this Book that shaped history, this Book that made America great, this Book that builds the church.

A billion Bibles. Enough New Testaments, end on end, to reach to the moon or to circle the globe twelve times.

A billion seeds! Indestructible seed. Potent seed. Seed God Himself guaranteed will grow (see Is. 55:11). Seed to produce fruit. Seed to revolutionize the human race. A billion seeds to bring joy and gladness, life and light, love and peace. A billion seeds that will bring man back to God his Creator.

Let this be the Day of the Bible. Let this be the time to fulfill our Lord's Great Commission. Let this be the moment to send the seed, so the reaping can begin, and the church enlarged in preparation for the return of our Lord.

The tools are available—the printing press, the computer, the telephone directory, the worldwide postal system—to finish the job.

We are seed-sowing specialists. We are enthusiastic about the billion Bible dream. But we dare not presume that only one method will accomplish the whole task.

The telephone is not yet available to the masses in some of the poorest countries. Millions do not yet know how to read. So the quickest and best answer for them may be the Bible on cassettes in their own languages. Gospel Records and Bible Translations on Tape are just two organizations God is using for this ministry.

Now is the time for the whole Body of Christ to use every available means to evangelize the world—by preaching, by teaching, by Sunday schools, by home witness, by television, by cassette players, by campus ministries, by prison outreaches, by relief programs, by neighborhood and office Bible studies, by personal witness of missionaries and national believers. Every appropriate method of modern technology should be harnessed for the gospel. Now is the time to utilize to the maximum the weapon of God's Word, which is sharper than any two-edged sword, more powerful than any nuclear reactor, and more penetrating than any laser beam.

My prayer is that every Bible-believing Christian the world over will be captured by the dream of giving every person on God's earth the Bible in his own language. Every Christian, regardless of country or station in life, rich or poor, young or old, can have a part in speeding God's eternal Word to the masses yet in darkness.

Just think what it would mean if every one of the over one billion professing Christians alive today would give just one Bible to each of four nonbelievers this year. Soon everybody on planet Earth would have the gospel. Naturally some in extreme poverty will not be able to do as much as others. But those who have more of this world's goods, especially people in America who God has blessed so abundantly, can do more. ". . . For unto whomsoever much is given, of him shall be much required. . ." (Luke 12:48).

I often wonder what might have happened if the Bible had been given to everybody in Russia before the seed of Marxism was planted in that land, or if the masses of China had received the Bible in their own languages before Mao Tse Tung's armies took control, or if more than two million Bibles had been distributed to the Chinese people before China closed its doors in 1950.

What if Bible distribution had been greater in Iran where the saintly Henry Martyn (whose motto was "Let me burn out for God!") translated the New Testament into the Persian language in 1811. He lived only one year after completing his great translation. Since Martyn's death, only 300,000 copies of the Bibles are known to have been provided for Iran. Only 300,000 in the last 170 years. What if 100 million Bibles had been made available to Iranians during just the past century? There might not have been a "hostage crisis." There might not now be a nation in turmoil with the potential of igniting the whole Middle East.

I am one of many Christians alarmed at the vast and terrifying world arms buildup. The nations are stockpiling weapons and building armies at a cost of over 500 billion dollars a year. Over half of that amount is being spent by the two super powers, the United States and the Soviet Union. There are already enough bombs to destroy the world ten thousand times over.

May God spare us nuclear holocaust. Even so, wars are now raging in the Middle East, Africa, Latin America, and Asia. Guns are firing and bombs exploding as I write this very sentence.

I think of an incident in World War II related by the veteran *Reader's Digest* journalist, Clarence Hall. As a war correspondent, Hall accompanied Allied soldiers advancing from one island to another during the closing months of the Pacific War.

On one assault, he followed American soldiers across Little Shimmabuke Island near Okinawa. As the advance patrol moved up to a village, two little old men suddenly stepped out, bowed low, and began to speak. An interpreter explained to the Americans that these were village elders welcoming them as fellow Christians.

The flabbergasted servicemen called up their chaplain. He and an escort toured the village and were astounded at the spotlessly clean homes and streets. The friendly natives looked incredibly healthy and showed evidence of prosperity and great intelligence. The Americans had seen other villages in the South Pacific, villages of indescribable poverty. The village of Shimmabuke shone among them like a diamond on a dungheap.

The headman, Shosei Kina, took the American's amazement for disappointment. "Sirs, we are sorry if we seem like such a backward people. We have tried our best to follow the Bible and live like Jesus. Perhaps if you will show us how. . . ."

"How did you get the Bible?" the astounded chaplain interrupted.

The headman recalled that thirty years before an American missionary had stopped briefly on the island, just long enough to make a couple of converts—the old men—leave them a Japanese Bible, and go on his way. They hadn't seen another missionary since.

One day the war correspondent and a tough old Army sergeant were stolling around the village. Compared to what he had seen on other islands, the grizzled sergeant just couldn't believe his eyes. "I can't figure it, fellow—this kind of people coming out of only a Bible and a couple of old guys who want to live like Jesus." Pausing, the soldier then delivered what Clarence Hall called "an infinitely penetrating observation." "Maybe," the sergeant said, "maybe we've been using the wrong kind of weapons to make the world over."

Surely, when so many billions are being spent for weapons of destruction to defend ourselves from enemies—

surely, when Christians in America can spend almost four billion dollars for brick and mortar in one year—surely, when we have at our disposal the means to speed the Word of God to the ends of the earth, surely we can rededicate our lives and accept the challenge given by David to Solomon: "Be strong and courageous and *get to work* . . ." (1 Chr. 28:20, TLB, italics mine). Surely we can give the Book of books to all who wait in darkness.

That is my prayer, my dream, my hope, my commitment, my life.

Having read this book, you may want to join in the excitement of sharing God's Word with the world. If so, contact:

Dr. & Mrs. Rochunga Pudaite
Bibles For The World
1300 Crescent, P.O. Box 805
Wheaton, IL 60187
Phone: (312) 668-7733